Anxiety Relief – Practical Guide

Mindful Meditation to Help you to Relieve Anxiety and Depression, Stop Worrying and Overthinking, Quiet your Mind and Change your Life

BEATRICE BECKER

© COPYRIGHT 2019 - ALL RIGHTS RESERVED.

TABLE OF CONTENTS

Mindfulness
for Anxiety

INTRODUCTION

Mindfulness is a word that, for some, has no genuine, strong definition. It's just fine to discuss focusing on your general surroundings; however, in actuality, how down to earth is that, truly? We experience a daily reality such that we're always associated—associated with work, to companions, to that person you met once in secondary school, and who infrequently loves your tweets. What great is it to sit and watch the spots you go each day when there's such a great amount of going on that you could be absent? The same number of individuals in this book would let you know, rehearsing mindfulness truly does a great deal of good. In a day and age when basically everybody is battling with some degree of uneasiness and sorrow, mindfulness can enable you to refocus. It can advise you that, odds are, you have all that you truly need. Furthermore, on the off chance that you don't, rehearsing mindfulness can assist you with accepting the truth of where you are currently and to advance toward what you need as opposed to enabling challenges and hardships to hinder you. Mindfulness is something other than checking out you and seeing things like the shade of the dividers and the vibe of the seat underneath you. Mindfulness is deliberately concentrating on where you are and what you're doing well now, and it's done in the little minutes. Do you have a terrifying regular checkup tomorrow? Power yourself to concentrate on the work you're doing now. Is it true that you are diverted by Facebook while having supper? Put the telephone down and make the most of your supper; focus on the interesting flavors and surfaces of the nourishment. Rather than awakening and promptly getting your telephone or beginning your morning schedule, take three minutes to sit, to inhale, to begin the day right. Permit yourself an opportunity to be simply. Reflection —the demonstration of sitting and concentrating on your breathing, of releasing contemplations and life for only a couple of moments of your day—can assist you with starting living with mindfulness, with beginning living at this very moment rather than one week from now and on the web. Be that as it may, genuine mindfulness happens when you're effectively living— when you're approaching your day. As you travel to work, keep your telephone in your pocket and notice things you don't typically focus on. What stores are around you at the stoplight? Is there a mystery park someplace that you never thought about? Is the sun warm and the sky blue, or is it shady and cold out? Glance around without judging. Will griping inside about the virus make the Earth tilt back toward the sun? Obviously not. Acknowledge the truth of what is. Try not to stop with your environment, however. Likewise, focus on what's going on in your very own heart and psyche. Enable things to be what they are. At the point when you're glad, clutch the feeling and truly feel it. At the point when you're tragic or focused, enable yourself to be dismal or pushed. Recognize the hardships you're looking as opposed to attempting to drive them where it counts inside the dim corners of your heart. In the event that you can enable reality to be what it is, on the off chance that you can enable yourself to be what your identity is, you can figure out how to acknowledge outrage and pity and afterward let it go. Start by giving yourself a couple of seconds to focus on what's near and inside you consistently. On the off chance that you can, take a shot at it simultaneously consistently. Be purposeful. Construct a propensity. Before long, you'll see that you're ready to concentrate on what you're taking a shot at somewhat more effectively. You'll wind up getting a charge out of the little, singular minutes that make every day one of a kind.

Furthermore, you'll have the option to relinquish things you never figured you could simply relinquish. Mindfulness isn't a get-well-snappy plan. It's another lifestyle.

CHAPTER 1: UNDERSTANDING ANXIETY

Difficulties are soul shaping… They can be lessons that lead us to know who we are… — Jean Shinoda Bolen, MD

Anxiety is an extraordinary battle, one that can chase after you for quite a long time and, at times, feel agonizing. But, incredibly, with the assistance of yoga rehearses, anxiety isn't just passable; it diminishes and turns out to be considerably less of an impact in your life. It's additionally one of those troubles that, when grasped and seen into, can give you who you really are. What's more, on the off chance that it does, it gives you a mind-blowing endowment.

As odd as this sounds, you're going to find that anxiety isn't the foe that it feels like.

Realize that, as somebody who experiences anxiety, you're not the only one. Numerous individuals have suffered it, ourselves notwithstanding, and it is anything but an individual imperfection to be on edge. We live in distressing occasions. Financial change, fear-based oppression, and worldwide warming undermine our aggregate presence. Despite the fact that your anxiety feels individual and is identified with your individual encounters, it happens with regards to nearby, national, and worldwide anxiety. We don't have the foggiest idea of how to determine the system anxiety, yet the numerous yoga rehearses talked about in this book can assist you with loosening up also, get to inward harmony. We likewise know, from our own understanding, that diminishing anxiety carries satisfaction to your life and energizes people around you. So as you center on your individual recuperating, breathe easy in light of realizing that your mending contacts the lives of others in a positive manner.

This book isn't just about anxiety; it's essentially about figuring out how to be quiet and placated. In spite of the fact that you've encountered anxiety, you've most likely to be loose, regardless of whether some time has gone since you felt that way. We're slanted toward unwinding in light of the fact that it's a characteristic state, one wherein we interface with ourselves and don't battle with life. Being loose doesn't make you aloof, uninvolved, or flippant. Or maybe, it enables you to make an amazing most and feel alright being you. Simultaneously, it helps make you rational and empowers you to settle on savvy decisions. Practice by training, bit by bit, minute by minute, yoga causes you to know what your identity is and be more quiet in your life.

Mary has a long history with anxiety, and qualities a lot of her recuperating to yoga. These practices proceed to consistent and quiet her when required, as the following story features. Mary used to have alarm assaults when flying industrially, so she was shocked numerous years prior, when we initially met, that she cherished flying with Rick in a solitary motor plane. Mary reviews: At an opportune time in our relationship, I began to look all starry eyed at Rick when he took me flying in a private plane. He was so upbeat up in the sky, moving with the mists. At that point, not long after our marriage, our funds changed; what's more, we never again had the additional cash for a plane. For quite a long time, Rick insightfully looked as planes flew overhead. Several years prior, our monetary circumstance improved. One day Rick called me from work and stated, "Hello Mary, I found a lot on a plane." I shivered with dread and addressed coolly, "What do we need are stores plane for?" Rick's voice fell, and he mumbled, "Alright." A month afterward, he called, and enthusiastically stated, "The cost for the plane has dropped generously; it's a super arrangement currently." Knowing that he cherished flying, I gulped my dread and reacted, "On the off chance that you need to purchase the plane, do it with my gifts." What I hadn't told Rick was that I was worried about being protected in the plane. I figured we would be more secure in the plane in the event that I additionally realized how to fly, so Rick is instructing me. While figuring out how to fly, I've felt extreme anxiety and even had a couple of mellow fits of anxiety, the first in more than a quarter-century. In any case, on account of my yoga rehearses, I had the option to inhale profoundly, center around what I was doing, and witness my troubling considerations. Subsequently, the alarm didn't absolutely overpower me. Grasping anxiety and relaxing through it gives me certainty, and now I'm now and then loose while flying the plane. Also, sharing Rick's happiness regarding flying is brilliant for me, and he's significantly contacted that I'm confronting my old dread of tumbling to my demise.

Encountering trepidation and anxiety is awkward, and in case you're similar to most individuals, you attempt to stay away from both. You become impervious to encountering them, wish they would leave, and would prefer not to realize them better or manage them. However, personally realizing anxiety disperses it, and this book tells you the best way to securely and bit by bit mend your anxiety. This first part contains a great deal of data about anxiety, since we've discovered that becoming familiar with it is a great initial phase in mending from it recognizing apprehension and anxiety

So you can truly comprehend what's happening inside you, how about we separate between the words "dread" and "anxiety," since they're regularly utilized conversely. Dread is the physical reaction to an outer danger. It's an instinctual, life-saving reaction to threat. Anxiety isn't a reaction to approaching threat. It's related to recollections of dread, expectation of dread, and maybe a natural inclination to being restless.

How anxiety really occurs in our bodies is stunning and complicated

As indicated by Joseph LeDoux in his article, "Enthusiastic Memory" (2007), enthusiastic encounters leave solid follows in our cerebrums. Through a procedure called dread molding, cells that procedure and transmit data in the apprehensive framework become molded, encoding the memory of dread and empowering apprehension to take on its very own existence in our bodies and brains. Along these lines, pondering a past terrifying occasion triggers the dread reaction in the present somewhat. For model, when you just recollect when you were excessively near a sheer drop-off, you feel the dread similarly as you did when you were really there.

Fear

You realize how incapacitating fear can be. Being looked with something you truly fear leaves you feeling immobilized, halted abruptly. By and large, you maintain a strategic distance from what you fear, regardless of whether it's creepy crawlies, snakes, statures, flying, swarms, shut spaces, open talking, being distant from everyone else, or innumerable different encounters.

Fear can keep you from accomplishing something you truly need to do. For example, in case you're scared of statures and wind up on the perception deck of a tall structure or at the Grand Canyon, where you need to step up to the handrail to investigate, you falter, swallow, and feel your heart pulsating. You remain back and wonder about, and maybe even feel desirous of, the individuals who go to the edge. Or on the other hand, perhaps you fix, summon your mental fortitude, and venture up. In any case, you're in the grasp of fear, which injects you with horrendous vibes that invade your experience of that minute. The tendency to remain back is reflexive and comprises of a bunch of exercises that incorporate vision changes, hormonal responses, physical reactions, considerations, and practices. Review a sheer drop from its summit causes a complex procedure to happen inside you in a small amount of a second. You become mindful; you get a shock of vitality, and your body solidifies. Apparently, in a similar glimmer, you react by speculation, wow! Subsequent to withdrawing or compelling yourself to go ahead, you may feel your heart pound and your hands tremble.

You've felt fear and how its remaining impacts persevere. Fear leaves an engraving, a type of physical molding that you deliberately and unwittingly store in your mind. In the wake of being in a circumstance that terrified you, related upgrades can reconnect the entire fear reaction. In that manner, fear lives on inside you. Looming peril triggers a reaction in the cerebrum and the body, one that is designed and intended to safeguard life. Called the battle or-flight reaction, it empowers you to run or make another move to spare your life. This is an instinctual, hormonal procedure that we share for all intents and purposes with the set of all animals. Or maybe than being exclusively a mental reaction, it's a complex neurophysiologic reaction including a few organs and zones of the mind.

Anxiety

Your experience of anxiety is the aftereffect of a circling exchange among a psyche distracted with wellbeing, nerve cells that translate life right now as being more hazardous than it is, and a body that fires up to flee or stand its ground. Here's the reason it might appear that you battle anxiety as well as experience it as a losing fight. The piece of your mind that procedures fear can't tell whether fear starts from your contemplations or from some genuine physical danger. In any case, your mind triggers the battle or flight reaction. As it were, your body responds to threat, genuine or envisioned, in the main way it knows how: with a major charge of vitality that sets it up to secure your life. Also, you aren't even mindful of what's going on, since this happens in the oblivious personality!

Firing up, your body, at that point, fills your fearful considerations. Maybe your body gives proof to your contemplations that there's something to be worried about.

The reactions of the body and the psyche enhance each other, and in that way, anxiety isn't just elevated yet, in addition, propagated. This leaves you in a condition of trouble, in any event, when, in all actuality, there's no real danger to your endurance!

Ideally, this little dialog causes you acknowledge why anxiety is so awkward. At the point when anxiety is a secret, it tends to dismay to manage; however, thinking about anxiety really builds the viability of the practices we educate in this book to mitigate it.

The Aspects of Anxiety

Anxiety has five avoidance:

- ➤ The habit of shirking
- ➤ An out-of-balance body
- ➤ Relived trauma
- ➤ The conviction that something isn't right with you
- ➤ The strong current

We should investigate them so you can perceive which of its perspectives relate to your experience of anxiety.

Propensity for Avoidance

One aspect of anxiety is the habit of evasion. The biggest fear is that of fear itself. Indeed, even being apprehensive is deadening: I would be excessively scared; I couldn't do it. No, I won't consider doing that! That would unnerve me to passing! I'm apprehensive it may hurt. At the point when Mary opposed purchasing a plane, she was propelled by evasion. The distress anxiety stirs an incredible helper, driving your decision to remain safe as opposed to go out on a limb. You most likely know this yourself, on the grounds that the greater part of us endeavor to abstain from encountering anxiety. Be that as it may, staying away from anxiety can deny you of building up your potential and of living completely. When your seen need to remain safe is vital, life shrivels, diminishing to hazard evasion, what's more, waiting be in charge.

Body Out of Balance

Another aspect of anxiety, a condition of substantial unevenness, is when anxiety stems from physiological causes. Unsettling influences in the cerebrum's substance delivery people and changing hormones in ladies' month to month cycles are two natural causes. Inner ear unsettling influences and a prolapsed mitral valve in the heart, causing what's known as "heart mumbles," may likewise cause anxiety.

Also, the body is delicate to what goes in it. What you ingest can cause anxiety. Caffeine, liquor, nicotine, professionally prescribed medications, cold cures, decongestants, diet pills, and certain recreational medications can cause anxiety.

Relived Trauma

Another aspect of anxiety is relived trauma. When remembering trauma becomes interminable, it's restoratively characterized as post-traumatic pressure issue. In case you're one of the a great many individuals who have endured past trauma, you may unknowingly re-create the fear reaction when a portion of your nerve cells translate what's occurring in your life today as the old trauma, and sign your cerebrum to plan your body to safeguard itself. This correspondence happens outside of your cognizant control, which implies that when this occurs, you aren't purposefully doing something incorrectly, and you aren't thinking your way into anxiety.

Trauma lives on in your body; it turns into a well-known encounter, only the way it is for your body. Trauma may sustain itself through dependence on adrenalin, which can lead you to take an interest in perilous, somewhat hazardous, or sensational practices (for example, betting, unbridled sex, savagery, or driving perilously) for the adrenalin surge that such encounters produce. At the point when the fear reaction feels typical, even alluring, to you, you'll search it out through such hazardous exercises. Trauma additionally lives on through reasoning self-deploring musings and acting on damaging motivations, which can appear as poor individual cleanliness, hanging out with individuals who aren't beneficial for you, utilizing self-talk that puts you down and taking part in a huge number of different harmful practices. These practices accidentally re-create the impacts of trauma, in this manner sustaining the fear reaction and keeping up an agonizing, endless loop.

Some kind of problem with's Me

Another feature of anxiety distrusting that some kind of problem with's you. This part of anxiety comes from misconception what your identity is. It's an instance of mixed up character. You believe you're blemished, by one way or another imperfect. This aspect of anxiety is established in convictions and thoughts regarding who you are as an individual. Here, it is your reasoning that causes anxiety, despite the fact that you may not know that you even have these contemplations. "I am not alright" is a bedrock conviction that fills the development of musings about being unable, for instance, I would never do that, and being unlovable, for instance, if I dissent, he won't care for me and may even relinquish me.

These contorting considerations live in the openings of your brain. Covered in the subliminal, they can begin whenever of life, in spite of the fact that we regularly partner them with interminable or intense youth injury or disregard. Since injury can be so wrecking to our bodies and brains, grown-up injuries can have a similar impact as youth injuries. At the point when you bring these considerations into cognizance (we tell you the best way to do this humanely) and see them for what they are, these bogus recognitions lose their capacity as oblivious helpers.

The gross misconception of what your identity is a ground-breaking reason for tension that is canvassed in a lot of detail later on in this book. For the time being, we're just presenting this feature of nervousness alongside different aspects.

The Mighty Current

This feature of nervousness, the compelling current, is a solid inclination of tension that is hard to classify. An incredible vitality, it pulls you under, and you feel as if you may kick the bucket. It feels like a fit of anxiety, yet has an alternate quality. Frenzy is heart beating, stunning, crude dread that is time-restricted.

This feels like a persevering current that sucks you under. Gigantic, it might ascend out of the aggregate oblivious, genealogical cell memory, a previous existence, kundalini (vitality of awareness that influences us mentally and profoundly), cultural tension, or a mix of these.

This amazing nervousness appears to ascend voluntarily. Not effectively represented, it appears to go with emotional meltdown, genuine inquiries of importance also, presence, and the profound developing voyage. It can appear during times of defenselessness, for example, physical ailment and individual change. This aspect of uneasiness isn't effectively verbalized at this point should be named. In the event that you've felt this current of uneasiness, you know it. This is the tension that takes you to the floor, where all you can do is inhale, remain cognizant, and give up.

Name Your Facet Of Anxiety

As you read through the features, on the off chance that you had the option to distinguish the kind of tension you ordinarily experience, you may think that its supportive of giving it a name. On the off chance that your nervousness appears to be excessively confounding or overpowering, at that point, return to this later in the event that you like. The thought here is to take a gander at your uneasiness and become more acquainted with it. You may perceive each of the five features in yourself; however, one may prevail. On the off chance that you recognize a prevailing feature, give it a name.

One companion named hers, "My Dearest."Her uneasiness was horrifying, despite the fact that natural and even "ordinary" for her. It had been with her for whatever length of time that she could keep in mind. At age fifty, after her mom's passing, she had a sense of security enough to look into her nervousness. Encompassed by the help of yoga classes, petition, composing, reflection, and calming yogic practices, she investigated this feature and recognized it as remembered injury. In the event that you give your tension a name, be delicate and understanding. Keep in mind, truth and sympathy are exceptionally mending. At the point when you genuinely become familiar with your aspect of uneasiness, your heart will dissolve. Obviously, you didn't mean or want to be restless. At the point when you perceive how it became, you see into yourself and your life.

You actually become progressively straightforward to yourself, and such lucidity is mending.

In outline, uneasiness can show itself and be knowledgeable about various ways. It will, in general, become constant and take on its very own existence. The impacts of nervousness can extend from mellow to serious, however negatively affect the body and mind, dissolving a mind-blowing nature.

Occurrence of Nervousness

As somebody who experiences nervousness, you may feel disconnected. With the goal that you understand how much organization you have, we should take a gander at the insights. The numbers shift; however, they all show that nervousness is inescapable in this nation. In 2005 R. C. Kessler, what's more, associates announced that roughly forty million American grown-ups matured eighteen and more seasoned, or somewhat more than 18 percent of individuals in this age bunch in a given year, have a diagnosable uneasiness issue

(Kessler et al. 2005). That is about one out of five individuals. A few people are on edge and don't have any acquaintance with it. When it gets incessant, you can get so accustomed to it that it feels typical.

Furthermore, numerous individuals discover approaches to work, notwithstanding nervousness. Exceptionally on edge, individuals may even appear to the outside world as quiet and placated. Various individuals have said to us, "No one understands that I'm this restless."

You And Anxiety

Despite the fact that nervousness is quantifiable and diagnosable, it stays a customized experience. Your nervousness is remarkable to you, and you experience it in your own way. Physically, you may have solid strain, fatigue, an annoyed stomach, what's more, a beating heart. Or then again perhaps you experience mental manifestations, for example, tireless stress, hustling musings, and troubling pictures, or have flashbacks of difficult scenes. Perhaps your nervousness shows on the enthusiastic level, making you feel bad-tempered, overpowered, or uneasy. Or then again maybe you surprise effectively, regularly checking nature and maintaining a strategic distance from possibly alarming circumstances.

Maybe you take no chances so you can stay in charge and abstain from going out on a limb. Possibly you have nonsensical feelings of trepidation that farthest point you. Anyway you experience uneasiness; it's what spurred you to get this book looking for alleviation.

Neuroscience And Nervousness

How about we go into a little science—not all that much, sufficiently only to give you a feeling of what occurs inside you when you're on edge. It will assist you with comprehension your body and will offer assurance to the yoga rehearses we instruct you.

Conscious And Unconscious Memory

A more critical see what occurs in your mind can assist you with acknowledging how tension is activated. In The Emotional Brain, Joseph LeDoux (1998) composed that the mind has two memory frameworks that are initiated by horrible memory. One memory framework stores cognizant recollections about the who, what, where, and when of the occasion. These are the subtleties you can review. Neuroscientists accept that these recollections are put away principally in the hippocampus (the piece of the mind answerable for learning and recalling) and parts of the transient flap of the mind. The second memory framework stores oblivious recollections about how your body reacted to past encounters, which are prepared by the amygdalae (which procedure dread) and the nerves that associate with them. (Recollect those nerve cells referenced before in part that procedure and transmit data?) This is the thing that triggers the thoughtful sensory system (part of the autonomic sensory system that gets dynamic during times of pressure) fight or- flight reaction, which you feel as dread. So as stunning as it sounds, it's definitely not what you intentionally recall that causes the heart beating and adrenaline surge that sign that your body is charged and prepared to do fight or flee.

You Can't Talk Your Way Out Of Fear

What you intentionally review and what your body recalls about injury originate from various pieces of the mind. These various wellsprings of data speak with one another; however, the associations running from the amygdalae (which, as recently referenced, process dread) to the cortex (which thinks and stores memories)are more grounded than from the cortex to the amygdalae. At the end of the day, the oblivious dread message, "Risk! Run for your life!"is not all that effectively interceded by the sensible reaction, "Gracious, it's not risky after all; there's a fence among you and the snarling protect dog."Even however you mentally realize that you're protected, the dread reaction proceeds: your hands shake, your heart pounds, and you continue looking behind you to be certain the pooch's still securely behind the fence. As you probably are aware, the dread reaction is essential to our endurance.

Its motivation is to keep you alive. In the brain, the amygdalae have four jobs:

> Get data from the outside world
> Decide its hugeness
> At that point trigger the dread reaction, if proper
> Send the message of dread to the cortex so you can survey the circumstance and choose what to do

When excited, it appears as though the battle or-flight reaction needs to work its direction out of your framework. In any event, the reasoning brain, or cortex, with more fragile associations with the amygdalae, has incredible trouble utilizing motivation to decrease exceptional feelings. This may clarify why it's so hard to diffuse extraordinary dread by guiding yourself to quiet down or that there's not something to fear. You can't talk or reason out of it.

Extreme Stress and the Brain

In Psychobiology of Posttraumatic Stress Disorder (2006), Bessel A. van der Kolk, a specialist on how extraordinary pressure influences the brain, clarifies how feelings are not the aftereffect of cognizant decision. The limbic brain structures, such as the amygdalae, decide feelings, just as the significance of what you see going on around you. In the event that they translate something you see, hear, or smell as risky, the outcome is an instinctual, hormonal reaction that sends a caution message to the brain. While you're not mindful that this inside procedure is going on, you're most likely mindful of the anxiety that outcomes, except if it's so natural to you that you're desensitized to it.

How about we take a gander at how flashbacks happen. Each of your amygdala stores memory, furthermore, if something helps it to remember a past injury, your body reacts in the equivalent way it did during the first occasion. This clarifies why, for the initial scarcely any months

in the wake of being back finished in a minor accident, you worry and hold your breath at the point when a vehicle behind you is delayed to brake at a stoplight. Mental pictures of past injuries we've encountered enact every amygdala, bringing about forceful feeling, and stifle every frontal flap, which hinders feelings and makes an interpretation of experience into words that can be expressed. Once in awhile, you're overflowed with feelings yet can't discover words to tell others what's going on. A comprehension of how the frontal flap gets smothered when the amygdala is initiated clarifies why it's so hard to express what's happening when you're profoundly vexed. The frontal piece of the brain understands emotions and driving forces. Notwithstanding, it doesn't appear to expel them, mostly in light of the fact that when we're focused on, the frontal projection territories get less bloodstream. Just a short time later, when you're never again strongly disturbed, bloodstream increment in your frontal projections, empowering you to understand and discuss what you encountered.

The Stress Response

Despite the fact that we've just discussed the pressure reaction, we'll characterize it here quickly so you can contrast it with the unwinding reaction. In 1915 Dr. Walter Gun instituted the expression "battle/flight' in his book Bodily Changes in Pain, Appetite, Fear, and Rage: An Account of Recent Researches into the Function of Passionate Excitement. This "battle/flight" reaction is likewise called the pressure reaction.

In particular, under Stress:

> ➢ Your heart thumps quicker, and your muscles tense.
> ➢ Your breathing gets shallow, and you begin to sweat.
> ➢ The progression of blood to your inward organs and limits diminishes.
> ➢ The working of your safe and stomach related frameworks is repressed.

At the point when you're restless, your body assembles for activity. However, with no compelling reason to flee, your body remains fired up, in a condition of caution. Our bodies are most certainly not intended to work under a consistent condition of pressure. After some time, the impacts of the stress reaction negatively affect your physical wellbeing, vitality, state of mind, and a general feeling of prosperity.

The Relaxation Response

But when you're in physical peril, your wellbeing and feeling of prosperity rely upon your body's unwinding reaction. Being loose is an entire body experience and was first portrayed by Herbert Benson in quite a while 1976 book, the relaxation response. The unwinding reaction decreases the pressure reaction, and, like the pressure reaction, is started in the brain. In particular, the unwinding reaction incorporates the accompanying:

> Your pulse backs off, and your circulatory strain balances out.
> Your invulnerable framework is supported.
> Your brain waves delayed down.
> Your stomach related procedures standardize.
> Your nature of rest improves.
> You experience a feeling of prosperity.

At the point when your body unwinds after you've been incessantly tense, you feel like yourself again or find another and wonderful feeling of simplicity. Your psychological working improves, and you truly "wake up"; that is, you become progressively mindful of what you're seeing, hearing, tasting, smelling, and contacting. Accordingly, you can think all the more obvious, and all the more precisely take in data from the outside world.

Anxiety and brain wave activity

You've without a doubt had times when your musings hustled so rapidly that they were deficient, tumbling more than each other and dominating the spot. This happens when you're on edge or truly energized, and it will, in general, destroy you.

Your brain's hecticness in making considerations is called brain wave action, and the pace at which you produce contemplations can be estimated. Brain wave movement is inspected through EEG (electroencephalograph) testing. At the point when you're on edge, your idea wave action is called beta waves, since you're creating musings at a mood of thirteen to thirty cycles for every second. At the point when you're loose, your brain wave movement is called alpha waves.

Thoughts slow down and take on a more coherent rhythm of about eight to twelve cycles per second. As noisy and worried thoughts subside, the mind becomes quiet, and you feel contented. Because your mind is less active, you can relate to what's actually going on, and you're more present for the current moment, the now.

Neuroscience, Exercise, And Healing

The body and the brain are amazingly touchy and flexible. They can be harmed by intense or constant pressure, and pivot and mend from its belongings.

What's more, you can facilitate the mending procedure along, as you're going to see. The brain is continually making new neurons. In 1998, Fred Gage and partners at the Salk Institute for Biological Studies found that we human creatures are fit for developing new nerve cells all through life, on the off chance that we physically work out (Eriksson et al. 1998). Physical exercise improves the development of new brain cells in the hippocampus, which, as referenced prior, is the piece of the brain that is fundamental for learning and recalling. This implies working out, strolling, and rehearsing the physical stances of yoga every day, not just work off collected worry in your body yet, in addition, help your brain.

Exercise is a basic part of your recuperating program. Here's the reason: Research has built up that pressure can harm the hippocampus. In Why Zebras Don't Get Ulcers, Robert Sapolsky (2004) announced that the hippocampus is defenseless to stretch. It has a higher thickness of receptors for the pressure hormone cortisol than practically some other region of the brain. At the point when stress is incessant, your hippocampus starts to contract. Stress verifiably negatively affects your body and your brain; however, you're not damned. You can intercede without anyone else sake.

Meditation Is Healthy For Your Brain

Science has clarified that physical exercise is, without a doubt, amazing medication. Be that as it may, there's a great deal more you can do to discover solace and wellbeing. Once more, how about we see research to perceive what it has illustrated. In Beyond Biofeedback (1977), Elmer and Alyce Green investigated examine led in 1970 at the Menninger Foundation in Topeka, Kansas, where they considered willful power over automatic states. A yogi, Swami Rama, changed his brain wave designs upon request. In thoughtful states, he willfully went from beta brain waves, related with dynamic idea, to alpha waves, related with unwinding, to theta waves, by and large connected with oblivious states. As it were, he backed his speculation way off, potentially like your involvement with the short-lived minute before rest.

The Menninger Foundation investigation of thoughtful states was not segregated. In 1966 A. Kasamatsu and T. Hirai confirmed the impact that reflection has on brain wave activity. Their EEG investigations of Zen meditators demonstrated that accomplished meditators go into theta brain wave movement. Concentrates on reflection are currently broad, as plot by Michael Murphy (1999) in The Physical and Psychological Effects of Meditation: A Review of Contemporary Research with a Comprehensive Bibliography, 1931–1996.

Because of the developing enthusiasm for reflection and the gathering proof that it's so bravo, look into has multiplied as of late. How about we survey what scientists are finding. In 2004 researcher Richard Davidson and partners provided details regarding EEG investigations of priests (Lutz et al. 2004). They found that electrical action was elevated during reflection in the left prefrontal cortex, just behind the temple. Expanded movement here is related to positive feelings. In 2007 Davidson and associates wrote about investigations indicating that long haul meditators have increasingly electrical flag in the brain related to focus and enthusiastic control (Brefczynski-Lewis et al. 2007). This shows that an act of contemplation prompts having increasingly positive feelings, and the capacity to think and direct feelings.

Sara Lazar is a neuroscientist who explores how reflection influences our brains. In 2005 she and her partners announced the discoveries of an investigation where they analyzed the brains of Western-style mindfulness meditators to those of non-meditators. They found that a continuous contemplation practice can advance solid cortical changes in grown-up brains in zones significant for intellectual and enthusiastic preparing and prosperity. Lazar accepts that different types of yoga furthermore; reflection would have a comparable positive effect on brain structure.

As such, contemplation is sound for your brain. Reflection can help invert the toll that pressure takes on your brain by improving fixation, helping you react in more advantageous manners to upsetting circumstances or stress, quieting you, and boosting your feeling of prosperity.

Breath and healing

The most clear and prompt approach to feel less on edge is by changing how you relax. Since breathing intentionally is so successful, we're presenting it here, in the main section, so you can quiet your nerves and calm your body at the point when you have to. We know by, and by that, we don't need to endure unnecessarily at the point when only a couple of full breaths can reestablish our prosperity. We depend on these breathing practices to help our joy. Not a day passes by that we don't take full breaths; similarly, we'll instruct you to do.

You can truly turn around your body's pressure reaction by changing how you relax. At the point when you're restless, center around taking moderate, full breaths to trigger the unwinding reaction. Here's the reason breathing has this impact: Breath is the main physiological capacity that is constrained by both the intentional and automatic sensory systems. Similarly, likewise, with the pulsating of your heart, the development of your breath is managed by the autonomic or automatic sensory system. You don't need to say, "Take in, inhale out deliberately."But in light of the fact that breath is moreover constrained by the willful sensory system, you can inhale purposefully. You can stretch and extend your breaths. Breathing intentionally is at the core of yoga rehearses and is a lifeline that balances out you when you're focused.

Practice: Breathing Intentionally

It's easy to experience how breathing intentionally works right now, as you sit there reading this book.

1. Breathe in through your nose and blow the air out through your mouth, as if you were blowing out a candle.
2. Now breathe naturally, in and out through your nose.
3. Repeat this process. Breathe in through your nose, and blow the air out through your mouth, as if you were blowing out a candle.

4. Now breathe naturally, in and out through your nose.
5. Continue breathing normally.

You just altered your breathing. Most likely, your breath is now a little deeper, a little more optimal. We do want to note here that in a truly relaxed and "present" state, you don't voluntarily focus on deep breathing; that is, you don't think about or control your breath.

However, when you're distressed, you can restore relaxed breathing with this breathing practice.

Deep breathing is optimal and is how you breathe when you're really relaxed. You've probably noticed how full and slow breath is when someone's in a deep sleep. Napping babies illustrate this wonderfully. Lying on their backs, babies have innocent bodies that are fully relaxed and soft bellies that rise and fall with the breath. Unless you've been trained in breathing practices, you probably don't breathe much of the time optimally. If you're among the fortunate few who do, you're probably a calm, clear-thinking person.

The Breath Of Anxiety

Despite the fact that breathing is represented by the autonomic sensory system, it's affected by the intentional sensory system. Constant anxiety and pressure capably condition the breath, to such an extent that occasionally, in any event, when we rest, our breath doesn't come back to ideal relaxing.

At the point when you're frightened, you wheeze and hold your breath, which triggers your body's pressure reaction with the goal that your heart pulsates quicker and your breathing rate increments. At the point when you're incessantly on edge, your breath stays fast and shallow, at any rate somewhat. Shallow, fast breathing and anxiety take part in a shut criticism circle of correspondence; that is, your anxiety triggers shallow breathing, and your shallow breathing triggers anxiety.

The breath of anxiety is a type of hyperventilation—which is quicker or more profound breathing, or both—that causes an abatement of carbon dioxide in your blood. It can cause tipsiness, deadness, or shivering in the hands or feet, discombobulating, chest torment, and slurred discourse. On the off chance that you have a fit of anxiety, hyperventilation is increasingly serious, and in the event that you experience the ill effects of constant anxiety, your breathing is most likely a mellow type of constant hyperventilation.

At the point when our breathing is loose, and we're solid, our breathing has a whiz development to and fro from breathing principally through one nostril to the other. In case you're solid, you exchange from right-to left-nostril strength roughly every a few hours. The autonomic sensory system, conceivably coordinated by the nerve center, is answerable for pivoting the breath from one nostril to the next. Anxiety changes this common musicality and causes drawn-out right-nostril relaxing. This fascinating truth features the sensitive interaction of our mind-sets, breathing, and physical body.

Breathe And Become Calm

You can reestablish diaphragmatic, or ideal, breathing by doing the accompanying practice. Before you start, we have a tip: Pay more regard for your exhalations than inward breaths, in light of the fact that the breath that pursues a full out-breath is consequently more profound. It takes just a couple of restorative breaths to reestablish ideal relaxing.

Work on: Breathing Slowly

1. Sit easily and center around your relaxing. You have two choices now: inhale through pressed together lips, as though you were whistling, or tenderly close off your correct nostril with your thumb also, inhale through your left nostril. Notice that you can't move as much air. The powerlessness to move as a lot of air starts to ease hyperventilation.

2. Hinder your breathing by taking into the tally of four and out to the tally of six for three full breaths. Try not to drive the breath.

3. Enable the breath to get more full gradually.

4. Presently continue ordinary relaxing.

5. After your breathing is progressively ordinary, practice tummy relaxing for a few moments. This will quiet you by enacting the parasympathetic unwinding reaction.

Practice: Belly Breathing

1. Sit comfortably or lie on the floor with your knees bent and your feet on the floor. Lying on the floor is usually more comfortable.
2. Place one hand on your belly just below your ribs. Place the other hand on your chest.
3. Pat your belly, and then pat your chest. You'll find this soothing.
4. Breathe in through your nose.
5. Exhale through pursed lips and feel the hand on your belly fall in toward your spine.
6. Breathe in through your nose and let your belly push your hand out away from your spine.
7. Focus on slow, relaxed exhalations.
8. Repeat these steps three to six times. Take your time and enjoy breathing.

Conclusion

Anxiety is exceptionally pervasive and has been contemplated widely. It includes the body's pressure reaction, and mending from anxiety includes enacting the unwinding response. Anxiety lives in your body and mind and can take numerous structures. Since your experience of anxiety is extraordinary to you, it gets to know precisely how it shows throughout your life. Realizing what anxiety does to you causes you to remember it with the goal that you would then be able to create powerful practices for recuperating from it.

Science has not just found the pressure reaction, and the unwinding reaction, however, has additionally checked how to reestablish a sound harmony between strain, what's more, unwinding. Regardless of whether anxiety comes from deduction or from a past injury, both body and brain are influenced, and recuperating requires quieting the body and calming the psyche. Yoga and reflection have been demonstrated to be priceless in doing both. We'll investigate reasons for anxiety to facilitate your comprehension of how and why anxiety lives in you.

CHAPTER 2: HOW THINKING MAKES YOU ANXIOUS

The product of extraordinary harm in early youth, disgrace makes us recognize with our impediments so as to not perceive our essential goodness or the conceivable outcomes we need to show the innovative capability of the human soul.

— Father Thomas Keating

Somehow, thinking ends up being uncovered as one of the main drivers of our anxiety. In spite of the fact that we're mindful that believing is in the blend, how it relates to anxiety can appear to be somewhat secretive. One explanation it's confusing is that we're regularly unconscious of the contemplations that assume a significant job in anxiety. They deal with us underneath our degree of mindfulness. The sorts of contemplations that fuel anxiety are those that reveal to us we're not commendable, that we're imperfect people. These excruciating considerations, which haven't the faintest idea about our essential goodness, seethe and touch off into anxiety, and have, for the most part, been with us since youth.

Another way thinking contributes is by heightening the subsequent anxiety when we're activated into a flashback. For instance, a veteran may have the battle or flight reaction of past battle experience when there's an uproarious blast, for example, at the point when an article has been dropped on the floor close by. At the point when this happens, no evident contemplations have made the anxiety, nor is there a real outer danger.

In any case, in the brief instant after the frightening, the veteran's psyche normally responds with musings like, What! Gracious, my God, what! which feed the dread. Also, discussing or recalling the old injury can trigger a flashback. Regardless what the first reason, regardless of whether it's natural or ecological, your brain responds to feeling restless such that will, in general, sustain and increment your anxiety, for instance, when you think, Oh, no, here it returns once more! in the wake of beginning to feel those natural apprehensive sentiments.

Thinking plays a major role in anxiety

How about we take a gander at where the musings that reason anxiety originate from. Frequently, they're programmed and recognizable, to such an extent that you're neglectful of them, think about them to be typical, or both. These are musings about who you trust you are. In the event that, as the product of youth injuring, you accept that you're a mediocre individual, you have a profound conviction that turns into an inevitable outcome. You bear it in your head for an amazing duration and experience the ill effects of the agony related to it.

Accepting a falsehood like that, one that says you're short of what others, is an underlying driver of anxiety.

Inferiority Complex

You've known about the term Inferiority Complex, which alludes to a solid hidden sentiment of individual inadequacy that as often as possible causes either restrained or then again forceful conduct, the last in overcompensation for the sentiments of inadequacy. Accepting that you're not skilled enough makes an absence of trust in your capacity to explore through life. You may maintain a strategic distance from hazard taking, and try to play it safe so as to abstain from inciting your anxiety. It's similar to fearing your very own shadow and thusly abstaining from going out in the sun. Thus, you may not feel restless; however, your reality turns out to be little, restricted, and stale. On the off chance that you accept that you're unlovable, you may feel apprehensive from thinking about whether you'll be abandoned, feel that others are insulting you, or dread abuse by those you live with.

On the other hand, you may have reacted to a feeling of being second rate by overcompensating for it. Numerous individuals lift themselves up by their own bootstraps. Through difficult work and unadulterated coarseness, they make themselves "great enough." If this portrays you, your endeavors most likely helped you along in your life. Nonetheless, you may have a chewing feeling that you're a fraud, and dread that others will discover that you're not as brilliant as you'd like them to think you are. You likely make a decent attempt and endeavor toward flawlessness. As opposed to trust your impulses and insight, you concede to models you've embraced. At that point, as a long time pass by, it might occur to you that you don't have any acquaintance with yourself. That is the point at which you may find the profound flows of anxiety that have lived in you for quite a while.

Assuming any of these portrayals fit you, read on so you can, finally, find who you are underneath your feeling of mediocrity.

Identifying with thoughts

Considerations are as private as your breath in that they live inside you and can influence each part of life. Contemplations are so close yet can't be seen and, by and large, live underneath the radar screen of your mindfulness. You have a lot more contemplations than you understand. Accordingly, the emotional effect that considerations have on your life is normally dark.

Maybe you have a mystery life in your reasoning personality that extends out into your cognizant world.

Huge numbers of the considerations that reason anxiety have their inceptions in adolescence.

They're as well-known in your inward scene as the movement of your relaxing.

They dwell out of sight of your mindfulness like the thundering sound of far off thunder. While musings may appear as innocuous as far off thunder, they're not. Oblivious considerations apply extraordinary impact. Contemplations can have an incredible sway, regardless of whether they've seen or oblivious. In this way, it's imperative to comprehend your association with your considerations.

You're More Than Your Thoughts

Basic to your capacity to decrease your anxiety is understanding that you're a lot more than what you might suspect. You can't be completely depicted, bound, or contained by the words you think or express. This is generally excellent news since it implies that no idea or thought verges on catching the substance of what your identity is. Figuring out that words don't characterize you is an immense understanding, one that encourages you to stop accepting words that reason you to feel awful about what your identity is.

Self-referential considerations are words that you think or state to depict yourself.

Regardless of whether they develop you or tear you down, such considerations are, best case scenario, mistaken and just a halfway articulation of what your identity is. The contemplations you hear may go from Something's the issue with me to I'm exceptional. Whatever the substance of your contemplations, they're a deficient definition or depiction of who you are. You can make a not insignificant rundown of all that you think portrays you; however you'll always be unable to make an absolutely adequate rundown. The substance of your contemplations doesn't characterize you, in light of the fact that the reasoning personality is just a single part of what your identity is. That, however, the reasoning personality is naturally constrained in its capacity to get a handle on the totality of what your identity is.

Even though you're immensely more than your thoughts, you unavoidably identity with them. As a result, when you say, "I am afraid," you momentarily identify with fear. The words "I am afraid "have a linking, bonding element to them. You identify yourself with what comes after the "I am," for example, "I am funny," "I am a genius," "I am sad," "I am terribly upset," "I am creative," "I am not creative," and so on. It's as if the words after "I am" are your name, which you relate to as if it's all that you are in the moment it's spoken.

Adopting a Story of Identity

The feeling of turning into a "someone," and "I am", occurs very ahead of schedule in youth. Call a four-year-old by an inappropriate name, and she'll likely let you know what her identity is: "I'm not Suzie; I'm Sue!" Identifying with your given name is an evident case of utilizing words to describe what your identity is.

While it's human instinct to character with contemplations as you build up, there's more to it. People are storytellers. Indeed, even as a kid, you recounted stories to yourself about what your identity is. Like each story, accounts of self-personality have topics. Stories about what your identity is flowing around two center topics, individual competency and adorableness. The subject of competency appears as varieties of "I'm brilliant," "I'm a moderate student," "I'm a triumph," "I'm a disappointment," "Things come effectively for me," and "Life's hard for me."The list is ceaseless. The topic of adorableness appears as varieties of "I'm cherished," "I need to gain love," "No one's there for me," "I have a major heart," "I need to deal with others so as to be cherished;" also, "I'm not alright as I am."

Your account of what your identity is depends on correlations with others. Truth be told, it's fundamental to have a reference point for correlation. Your brain evaluates your story of character by how you feel your own characteristics contrast or stand out from those of others:"I'm more brilliant than my sibling." "I'm calmer than different children," "I'm better known than most," or "I'm the favored offspring of my mom."

Accounts of personality depend on your individualized encounters of conditions and connections that happened during adolescence. These accounts live on in your mind until and except if you perceive the truth about them: stories that you clutch in your brain. This implies except if you become mindful of the narratives, complete with subjects, frames of mind, and convictions about what your identity is, you unknowingly live them out throughout everyday life. Much anxiety comes from these self-constraining stories that you made in youth, particularly those accounts that you framed around injury and difficulty.

Why Your Story Matters

To develop and to beat anxiety, it's fundamental that your old tales about who you thought you were gotten straightforward to you. At the point when you become aware of old stories, they start to lose their vigorous grasp on your life. At that point, when you understand that some old story is influencing your life, you can react with, "Stunning, it's that old story once more."

When you see a major pothole in the street, you can back off or drive around it. In a similar way, when you become mindful of your old story, it doesn't have a similar effect on or control over your life. In the event that you don't see your story, you stall out in it again and again once more. Note that we're not prescribing that you stay away from your story; we're proposing that you become more acquainted with it and see how it influences you, so it doesn't keep you caught in the regular old anxiety-creating grooves. Shockingly, a great many individuals accept accounts of character that drag them down. In the event that your story reduces you in any capacity, it can drive you into a few agonizing and upsetting spots. For instance, if your story is tied in with being unlovable, you may wind up seeing someone where you're not supported or in the way of life or then again profession that is not expressly satisfying. Remembering "I'm sufficiently bad," stories can dissolve your wellbeing and make a lot of anxiety and enduring.

The aftereffects of a significant investigation of more than 17,400 center salary people led at Kaiser Permanente HMO in San Diego confirmed that unfavorable youth encounters happen significantly more as often as possible than is for the most part recognized. In the examination, detailed by Dr. V. J. Felitti and associates (1998), 50 percent of the respondents detailed having survived difficulty in right on time life. Unfavorable youth encounters were classified as pursues: adolescence passionate, physical, and sexual maltreatment; enthusiastic or physical disregard; seeing abusive behavior at home, or parental partition or separation; and growing up with drug-abusing, rationally sick, self-destructive, or criminal family individuals. It's critical that half of the center pay respondents announced having seen or experienced excruciating encounters as kids. This investigation makes it evident that injury and troubles are inescapable and cross every financial line. The effect of unfriendly youth encounters was additionally canvassed in the investigation. Of course, the more noteworthy the quantity of unfavorable circumstances experienced in youth, the more critical the impact. The impacts extended from anxiety, misery, and liquor abuse to physical medical issues and even unexpected passing. Prior to proceeding, we need to include some point of view. Individuals react contrastingly to affliction, and early life conditions don't consequently decide your destiny. Your youth encounters themselves don't really decide the story you enlighten yourself regarding yourself. At any rate, there's not a one-to one connection between the two. A great many individuals originate from appalling childhoods; however, they set up their accounts together in various manners. For instance, three siblings can experience childhood in practically the equivalent brutal and injurious family, be that as it may, turn out with altogether different stories due to their individualized methods for assembling their encounters in their psyches. Significantly more dominant than what transpires are the accounts you accept about what occurred. We've examined how injury lives on in the body. Here we're focusing on that stories live on too. In the event that you think little of the impact of your initial youth on your present life, ignoring the intensity of old convictions, you may remember anxiety for quite a long time to come and not live completely. To break the cycle of anxiety, it's basic to look profoundly into the idea of the old center stories that reason anxiety.

Conditioned Self-Identity

The tales that you accept depict you are known as the conditioned self-identity.

You assimilated these thoughts from nature around you, and as such, they're outside to you in that what you heard didn't begin in you. For model, if a small kid is reliably informed that she's not as keen as her sibling, she normally factors her elucidation of that announcement into her story about how keen she is. We know numerous brilliant individuals who accept they aren't savvy enough; you presumably do also. However, in all reality, none of us can be decreased to what our folks said or didn't state about us. In a similar way, you can't be characterized by what did and didn't transpire. While you were effectively affected by youth occasions in that whatever you encountered lives on the grounds that it turned into a piece of the narrative of you, what occurred in those days doesn't verge on depicting the full truth of what your identity is.

You may think you've abandoned the past, and in certain regards you have.

However, except if you've altogether analyzed your accounts, your methods for managing feelings, your relational examples, your techniques for progress and disappointment, and your methodologies forgetting or dismissing love, you accidentally propagate the stories that emerged out of your initial life. Except if there's a huge move of cognizance, your feeling of identity originates from how you were raised.

Practice: Explore Your Story of Identity

Become familiar with your account of identity by finishing the accompanying sentences:

> ➤ I'm the sort of individual who ________________.
> ➤ I've generally accepted that I was ________________.
> ➤ I depict myself as self-worth

Lamentably, huge numbers of us accept that we need to acquire or fabricate self-worth, not realizing that we're innately important unimaginable. Numerous guardians don't acknowledge how valuable their youngsters are, not on the grounds that they're heartless or untalented guardians but since they don't have the foggiest idea about that, all human life is valuable. Somewhere inside, they don't feel that their very own lives are holy. Just when guardians realize that they themselves are absolutely valuable "in light of the fact that," can they completely transmit that message to their kids. On the off chance that they didn't get that message from their folks or on the other hand, find it all alone, they have no plan of action yet to accept their elucidation of their molding and unwittingly give to their youngsters what was passed down to them. What gets passed on, age after age, is a misconception about self-worth, that it's restrictive rather than unequivocal.

Intentionally or unknowingly, we want to know and experience ourselves as entire and commendable. This longing may persuade you, as it does innumerable others. Not realizing that you're as of now entire may cause you to respond by embracing some anecdote about what a decent individual resembles and afterward demonstrating your life as per how you figure you ought to be. You redress for not realizing your consecrated worth by making yourself into what you think you ought to be.

Betty's Story of Identity

I was brought up in rustic New York by my separated from mother, who was rationally sick. My mother feared water and precluded us from going close lakes. Right up 'til today, I'm alarmed of profound water. It's my mystery; even my spouse of thirty years and two little girls don't have a clue. I'm so embarrassed; being not able swim shows my destitution. I don't need individuals to realize that I was raised as a poor young lady. I set off for college and wedded all things considered, and I've endeavored to develop myself. I don't need anybody to realize that I can't swim, so I make up persuading deceives dodge the water.

Betty unavoidably accepted that what her identity was mirrored her childhood, as we as a whole do. Having little feeling of being a significant, valuable individual, she was related to being horrendously poor, as though that were what her identity was.

The feature of anxiety she showed was, "A major issue with's me." Even however she's knowledgeable and affluent, she relates to a central story of being short of what others. She encountered three unfavorable youth encounters: parental separation, her mom's psychological instability, and psychological mistreatment. Betty made up for her resultant imperfect feeling of self by turning into a self-made lady. She moved on from school with distinction, keeps up a perfect appearance, and attempts to be an incredible companion.

In any case, she experiences incessant anxiety and fits of anxiety, not simply since she fears that somebody will get some answers concerning her adolescence however since, disregarding her valiant endeavors to make herself into a sufficient individual, she unwittingly accepts, as she did as a blameless little youngster, that she's not as commendable as others.

Primary Perspectives

Betty, similar to you and every other person, grew up and propagated her conditioned self and its accounts by observing self, others, and the world through the essential points of view contained in her center story. Her story was, "On the grounds that I was raised poor, I'm not on a par with others." The essential points of view become sifted focal points that you see out of. Since these focal points are twisted observations, you try not to consider yourself to be others as they seem to be. The point of view "Something's incorrect with me" is unavoidable and communicated in expressions, for example, "dislike others," "For what reason wouldn't I be able to resemble him?" "I would never do that," and "It never works for me."

These viewpoints shading your reality contrarily and contribute powerfully to anxiety.

"Some kind of problem with's Me" and the Fear of Public Speaking

At the point when, profound inside, you believe you're not alright, pressure results, which may cause you to depend on consolation from others that you're alright and brief you to decipher looks from others as basic. This difficult blend of requiring endorsement and seeing objection makes you keep down, for fear of treating it terribly, and is a underlying driver of social anxiety, the most predominant anxiety issue in the United States, as indicated by R. C. Kessler and associates (2005), who announced that 15 million American grown-ups matured eighteen and more established, or about 6.8 percent of individuals in this age gathering, have social fear. Fear of open talking is filled by the fear that the group of spectators will pass judgment on you adversely or that you'll make a trick of yourself. You stress that your deficiency will be uncovered and that addressing a gathering will mortify. Fear of open talking exhibits that you do not just observe apparently through your essential points of view yet in addition, internally. The focal points misshape vision the two different ways. In the event that you see others as making a decision about you, you, moreover, judge yourself. In the event that you amplify your flaws, you consider others to be amplifying your deficiencies.

In the event that you consider the idea of open talking frightening, you're not damned.

You can look at the center stories that fuel this fear. As you're going to find, you don't need to take a gander at life through the regular old perceptual focal points

Innocent Misunderstanding

What pursues are two truly engaging practices that empowered us to talk before gatherings, and they can help you also. To survey, anxiety about open talking is prodded on by a gross misunderstanding that leaves your tale about yourself. You actually think something false that causes you anxiety. You can clear up the misperception by making two mending strides. The initial step is to recognize your old story of personality. The subsequent advance is to call it by its actual name: "innocent misunderstanding."

Practice: Continue Exploring Your Story of Identity

What's your old story of the sort of individual you are? Become more acquainted with it well with the goal that it never again influences you unwittingly. To proceed with your examination, here are five additional sentences to finish:

> ➤ The greatest falsehood I've accepted about who I am is ____________.
> ➤ What I don't need others to think about who I am is ____________.
> ➤ Somewhere inside, I generally thought I was ____________.
> ➤ My folks thought I was ____________.
> ➤ Summarizing it, an expression that best depicts the sort of individual I am is ____________.

Practice: Innocent Misunderstanding

Peruse what you wrote in the past training.

After each sentence, delay, inhale profoundly, and state so anyone can hear, "Old, old story, such an innocent misunderstanding." You may state "such an innocent misunderstanding" unlimited occasions. Let's assume it at whatever point you hear the old center story or feel it showing in your life. Each time you do this, you bring all the more recuperating. You recuperate since you talk reality. Your adapted character is the innocent misunderstanding of a youngster.

Conclusion

Your old story of what your identity is has an extraordinary impact on you. It lives on in your intuitive personality, underneath your mindfulness, as a reason and perpetuator of your anxiety. In any case, you're not bound to experience your days accepting old stories and remembering past difficulty. The recuperating practices of yoga assist you with perceiving how your mind capacities, give you incredible solace, and associate you with your inward quintessence.

CHAPTER 3: HOW YOGA HEALS ANXIETY

This act of witness is pure. It does not strive to be kind; it is just a good companion. And out of this companionship arises compassion.... We accompany our own pains and thoughts and hopes, whatever arises in the mind and heart—and notice kindly, as if what arises were a child, a lover, our oldest friend. — John Tarrant

When you start investigating the old stories that add to anxiety, you're on your approach to recuperating. It doesn't take a lot of searching for you to acknowledge how much enduring those innocent misunderstandings cause. Simply thinking about them is a consolation, and rouses you to keep peering inside. You understand how unconscious you were of the wellspring of your agony, and you comprehend in a very individual way what Socrates implied when he stated, "An unexamined life isn't worth living."

Becoming conscious

To help your internal looking, we'll talk about what happens when we look inside ourselves. To condense John Tarrant's remarks in the section opening epigraph, witnessing is an approach to be in association with ourselves. You become the person who's seeing just as the person who's encountering. At the point when you observe an extraordinary artist in front of an audience, you're in association with another person. At the point when you see your unhinged move of hurrying here and far off, you're in association with yourself. While you're really watching another person, you overlook yourself, and while you're really watching yourself, you get yourself. It might even invite you to state, "Here I am, hustling around." Then a fascinating thing is probably going to occur. You may wind up backing off. Just becoming mindful mitigates you. Witnessing is the means by which you become mindful.

The Practice of Witnessing

Witnessing is the capacity to watch musings, feelings, physical sensations, what's more, vitality—all the action that goes on inside you. Witnessing is paying thoughtfulness regarding yourself as you do when you're mindful of your environment. You figured out how to watch traffic when you drive, watch over your kids at play, or watch out for the stove when you're preparing a supper. Despite the fact that you learned step by step instructions to concentrate, your capacity to watch is an intrinsic limit. You can likewise figure out how to focus on what's going on in your inward world. You develop this limit through practice.

Practice: Simple Witnessing

Check out where you are at the present time. Notice the hues and shapes. Look at something intently, seeing its hues, shapes, or surfaces.

Presently put your consideration on yourself. Rub two fingers together and sense that. Respite and relax. Note the impression of your rear end on your seat. Respite and relax. Presently see the vibe of your heart's pulsating. Put your consideration on your condition once more. Take a gander at the hues, shapes, and surfaces that encompass you.

Move your consideration inside once more. Notice the vibes of the bottoms of your feet on the floor.

Look at your hands and notice the impression of vitality beating through them. Notice how agreeable this practice is! Your brain becomes assimilated in witnessing and thinks that it's pleasurable. Notice that there's no judgment in witnessing; it's unadulterated taking note. It's one thing to take note in any case, unquestionably all the more recuperating to see that you're taking note. In this practice, you were conscious that you were witnessing.

The Practice of Conscious Breathing

At the point when your breathing unwinds, so does your body. One approach to slow your breath is to inhale profoundly purposefully. Doing as such triggers the unwinding reaction and is an enormous drug for anxiety. At the point when you inhale consciously, your breath turns into a stay that keeps you from being diverted by anxiety.

Another approach to loosen up your breath is to focus on it. Basically, taking note of your breath without proposing to extend it tends to relieve, on the grounds that when you witness your breath, you don't focus on your reasoning. Your consideration is busy with breathing, and your psyche turns out to be calm. In this way, an amazing practice is essentially putting your mindfulness on your breath: breath coming in, breath going out, breath coming in, and breath going out. In case you're a hurrier, you may have skirted the last sentence. On the off chance that you did, it's alright; simply take note that you did. On edge minds do will in general surge. Attempt it once more: breath coming in, breath going out. At the point when you, in reality, delayed down and practice, you feel more quiet.

The Practice of Inquiry

At the point when you feel restless, the majority of your consideration is busy with hustling considerations and frightful sentiments. Those exceptional sensations are your essential state, what you most relate to. Inside, you don't simply feel that you're encountering anxiety, you feel that you are anxious. Be that as it may, when you ask into anxiety, it turns out to be all the more an optional state, or possibly an essential mutual state. You never again experience yourself exclusively as anxiety. You become an individual who's encountering anxiety however who is moreover asking. Relate to being a specialist of your experience, and interest turns into your essential state. You, as an intrigued individual, are examining anxiety. This diverse perspective encourages you to abstain from losing all sense of direction in anxiety. More than a restless individual, you're currently an individual having anxiety and finding out about it.

The practice of inquiry helps make you mindful that you're more than what you experience. You, a conscious being, have encounters and can realize what causes these encounters. Inquiry causes you to comprehend your inner universe of sensations, feelings, intentions, and observations. It likewise encourages you to get to the base of how you sustain anxiety. An extraordinary method to look underneath your surface encounters, inquiry is an examination concerning how your mind capacities, how your convictions sway you, and how your past encounters recover themselves. Perusing this book causes you to ask into anxiety so you can address it and not underestimate your standard experience. You previously made an inquiry when you investigated your account of personality and finished the sentences about your convictions about yourself. There are a lot more sentence-culmination practices in the book. We urge you to be interested as you work through these practices, getting out old bogus misunderstandings and revealing reality with regards to who you truly are.

The Practice of Practicing

We people are animals of propensity. Propensities, for example, anxiety become programmed furthermore, profoundly dug in through redundancy. While we structure a significant number of our propensities inadvertently or unconsciously, we can likewise create propensities deliberately. Yoga practices will assist you with developing new propensities, similar to how to manage anxiety rather than be constrained by it. The aggregate impact of a shrewdly chosen customary yoga practice is that you appreciate life more and can go out on a limb, and in case you're on edge, in any event, it isn't incapacitating.

Mary's Story

Mary experienced anxiety for a long time. In the wake of visiting yoga classes for two or three years, the more profound practices of breath mindfulness, witnessing, and heart contemplations flourished and started discharging anxiety's grasp on her. This story tells how rehashed practice calms anxiety:

A couple of years back, I started showing classes and going around the nation. Voyaging alone wasn't simple for me. I'm directionally hindered and get turned around effectively. I don't care for being lost, and I become alarmed. My mind gets silly, accepting that I'll be lost for eternity. On account of yoga practices, I presently perceive my trouble at the point when I'm driving in new places, inhale profoundly to stay in the present minute, do a rude awakening on my troubling contemplations, and discover my direction. I travel around the nation alone, not generally easily, yet dread doesn't stop me. On one excursion, I chose to pursue complex bearings and advance in my rental vehicle over the city to a café. While driving, my well-known frightening musings sprung up:

Imagine a scenario where I can't discover my way back to the lodging. This is excessively hard. This is befuddling. I ought to never have left the lodging. My autonomic apprehensive framework fired up, and I felt on edge. Simultaneously, I saw my considerations and concentrated on taking full breaths: take in, inhale out, take in, inhale out. Thinking returned and I could do a reality check: Look, you're not lost. You have a GPS and a mobile phone. It's sunshine. I practiced consoling self-talk: It's alright, you're alright. I made it to the eatery and requested a table in a calm region. Once situated, I started the alleviating yoga practice of putting my hand on my heart. I inhaled completely, sensed into my heart, and felt the glow of sympathy. Feeling upheld, I saw, in a new and profound way, how dug in those old frightful considerations were. Profound notches in the unconscious; they've been there for quite a while. I sobbed concealed tears, acknowledging by and by how inescapably dreadful contemplations have tormented me. I felt adoring generosity toward this molded character.

Wonderfully, from that point forward, dread hasn't overpowered me when I've been in new urban communities. Be that as it may, on the off chance that it emerges once more, I realize I have the backing of breath mindfulness, cherishing consideration, and the mental stability that originates from witnessing contemplations and feelings. The recuperating practices of yoga can change your relationship to anxiety, just as they've done and keep on accomplishing for Mary. Build up the practice of practicing. At that point, when anxiety grasps you, these practices are inserted in you, prepared to serve.

The Five Limits of the Mind

You can't manage what you're unconscious of. One of the incredible advantages of the practice of witnessing is that you become conscious of your psychological action. So that you can really do as such, it's useful to recognize what you're taking a gander at. This area gives you a few pointers.

Maybe when you were a youngster, somebody indicated out you the star groupings in the night sky. Remaining alongside you, possibly somebody raised a hand and called attention to the Big Dipper and the Milky Way. At that point, since you recognized what to search for, you saw them just because. When you could remember them, the experience of taking a gander at the stars got one of pleasure. So that you realize what to search for, yoga has laid out the five limits of the mind, making it feasible for you to investigate your mind and call your considerations by their actual names. Doing so is as satisfying as naming star groups of stars in the night sky, since what was once dark presently gets clear.

As per the yoga custom, the working of the grown-up mind is separated into five limits:

1. *Memory*
2. *Imagination*
3. *Perception*
4. *Sense of identity*
5. *Intelligence*

Memory

One of the elements of your mind is to store and recall data. Memory enables you to review where you live, where you work, which bank account is yours, and your favored nourishments. While memory is significant for sound living, being engrossed in the memory removes you from the present minute, and arranges your present life to occasions before. Feeling the pull of the past is anything but difficult to encounter. Here's a memory about graciousness:

I recollect my sweet German shepherd. Numerous years prior, one especially enthusiastic day, I sat in my chair, crying. My cherished eighty-five-pound hound slithered up on my lap and started licking my tears and crying. Moved by her empathy, I embraced her, and my tears died down. Composing now, I feel the passionate pull of the memory. She was a magnificent ally for me.

On the off chance that you like, attempt it yourself. Draw up a memory of generosity. Feel its impact on you. Notice how it pulls at you, and, for a moment, you disengage from the show and return in time. Abide for some time in that understanding, and afterward come back to the present minute.

Imagination

The human mind likewise has the capacity of imagination. A magnificent limit, it's the methods by which extraordinary music, workmanship, advancement, and funniness develop. However, your imagination can terrify you by concentrating on what may be. At the point when you're distracted with what's to come, you're surviving your imagination. You're consumed in what may occur and aren't focusing on the present minute. Being focused on what's to come is a trademark normal for anxiety. It doesn't make a difference whether what's to come is the following minute, day, or week, or years from now. Living, later on, is additionally simple to encounter. Here's a model:

I'm anticipating an ideal occasion, a get-together with two or three sweet nieces. We haven't seen each other for over a year. They're very dear to me, and I'm anxious to embrace them and invest energy with them. Composing presently, I'm grinning in expectation, since I love them so!

Attempt it yourself. Foresee some ideal occasion that you're anticipating. Feel its impact on you. Notice how it pulls at you, and, for a moment, you disengage from the present and move into the envisioned future. Presently, return to the present minute!

Perception

One of the elements of your mind is perception, which is the means by which you take in information from outside your body. You utilize your senses to learn from the physical world around you. Have an immediate encounter of how you take in data:

1. Put everything on hold and take a gander at shading in your quick condition.

2. Presently tune in to the sounds around you.

3. Taste any waiting flavor in your mouth.

4. Smell fragrances on your garments and hands.

5. Touch and feel this book.

Perceptions are much of the time distorted on the grounds that we translate the crude information coming in through our senses through the channels of our convictions and endurance impulses. Unavoidably, the considerations that underlie anxiety distort perception. Here's an undeniable model: If you accept you're ugly, then you're probably going to believe that others consider you to be unattractive. At the point when somebody turns and takes a gander at you, you accept that they're making a decision about you adversely. Your eyes take in information, and afterward, the information experiences the channels of the adapted mind. Your anxiety is brought about by how you decipher being taken a gander at, not the way that somebody sees you.

Sense of Identity

Another capacity of the mind is to build up an identity, a sense of "who I am." This empowers you to encounter yourself as an unmistakable person. Slowly, your sense of what your identity is becomes imbued and unchallenged.

Indeed, even your name isn't who you are in your pith. It was given to you. Your name is a word related to you that says nothing regarding who you truly are.

Obviously, substantially more than your name goes into your sense of identity. The point here is that even your given name is a part of your molding.

At the surface level, you may find that your self-identity has changed and become more positive. In any case, truly, the old story stays immaculate by your efforts to make yourself worthy. Improving your evaluation of yourself through great deeds and positive words resembles covering up old wood. Painting ensures the surface and looks great, yet underneath, the wood stays unaltered.

In spite of the fact that it might make you feel better to cover up the old story, the most profound mending originates from perceiving that your story isn't what your identity is anyway. It's not off-base to build up a story of what your identity is; it's a characteristic capacity of your mind. However, it's only one part of your mind, not the totality of who you are. At the point when you get this, you start to liberate yourself from the hold of your stories. When you figure out how to perceive your core stories, they don't have the regular old attractive draw on you, despite the fact that you may, at times, get sucked in for some time. Despite everything we do, and afterward, at some point or another, it occurs to us that we're made up for lost time in the undertow of our old stories. When we become aware, we see our stories for what they are, innocent misunderstandings, rather than accept they're what our identity is.

Intelligence

The mind has another capacity: intelligence. In the West, we ordinarily think of intelligence, or IQ, as a gathering of limits that can be estimated by target testing. The form of intelligence we allude to here is better comprehended as wisdom, and could likewise be called understanding, clarity, and knowing. You can't force wisdom or inward knowing. It just emerges or springs up, often when your mind is calm. For instance, you most likely once in a while, grapple with an issue in the evening when you're depleted. In your weakness, you can't choose what to do.

At long last, you surrender and express something to yourself like, "Good despondency, this is accomplishing nothing for you. Simply go to bed."The next morning, the answer for the issue occurs to you and appears glaringly evident.

Giving your reasoning a chance to mind enjoy a reprieve from your issues makes such great sense. You definitely realize you don't settle on your best choices when you worry and fuss, which, by and large, adds up to similar reasoning considerations over and over. Discover approaches to calm your mind with the reflection practices, and the appropriate responses you access will be undeniably shrewder than the ones that worrisome considerations create.

Become Aware of How the Mind Functions

At the point when you go on a long vehicle trip, a guide causes you to distinguish where you are.

Yoga causes you to perceive where you are in your mind by showing you how the mind functions and how to observe it. You can become aware of your mind's internal workings. With practice, you can observer having a memory, envisioning the future, or rehashing nothing new of identity. What's more, as you encountered in the witnessing practice prior in part, witnessing is social. You, the witness, become an ally to you, the scholar and experience.

This is really promising. At the point when you can perceive what your mind is doing, you don't thoroughly relate to your contemplations. You aren't as devoured by them, so you don't make yourself as insane. Being driven by subconscious considerations resembles driving around evening time with your headlights off.

You can't see where you're going. On the other hand, with your witnessing lights on, you can perceive what's happening inside your mind that causes anxiety, and you never again indiscriminately proceed down the equivalent excruciating street.

Practice: Explore Your Potentiality

Set aside some effort to interruption and focus your awareness in your body. Become aware of your body. Feel your hip bones on your seat and your feet on the floor. Feel your spine ascend out of your pelvis.

Loosen up your shoulders. Loosen up your jaws.

Become aware of your energy. Notice your breath come in and out of your noses. Presently see breath come into and out of your chest. Presently see that breath moves into and out of your paunch. Make the most of your breath!

The Five Sheaths

In yoga, sheath is a term used to portray the various layers of our being. Often contrasted with the layers of an onion, the length from our more shallow and clear physical body to the more subtle and more profound "bodies" of the feelings, mind, and soul. These sheaths acclimate you with your inward scene and assist you with distinguishing and guide out what you experience and where you experience it.

This is generally useful as you become more aware of your contemplations, feelings, and energy that correspond to anxiety and those that correspond to being mollified.

Next, we talk about the five sheaths, starting with the furthest and finishing with the deepest:

1. *Nourishment sheath*
2. *Energy (or prana) sheath*
3. *Mental sheath*
4. *Subtle (Buddhi, or wisdom) sheath*
5. *Happiness sheath*

The Food Sheath

The peripheral body is the nourishment sheath. Otherwise called the physical body, it's the fragile living creature and bones that make up the body you abide in. In spite of the fact that you live in the body, you aren't bound to it. You may distinguish essentially with your body, even decide confidence dependent on how you judge its relative magnificence. However, the tissues that make up your organs, skeleton, and muscles are just one measurement of your being. Tissues are transient and consistently evolving. The cells that contain the body consistently recover.

The Energy, or Prana, Sheath

The energy body, or prana, is the development of energy through your physical also, mental sheaths. Life doesn't exist without prana; we rely upon it to move our physical bodies, siphon blood, digest nourishment, breathe, think, and concentrate. We experience energy on a continuum of power, from exceptional to dormant. The pressure reaction works up prana and makes energy obstructs in the body. You comprehend what that resembles. Your heart pulsates rapidly; your muscles beat with energy, prepared to make a move; and your mind concentrates pointedly. In the event that there's no compelling reason to battle or escape, or there's no quick discharge for the repressed energy, your mind shifts from a particular concentration to hustling contemplations, and your body becomes unsteady or tense.

The unwinding reaction quiets your energy. At the point when the parasympathetic apprehensive framework is enacted, your mind becomes calm. Your pulse backs off, your processing improves, your physical body feels calm, and you experience a sense of prosperity.

Yoga works with prana basically through breathing activities and physical stances. Developing and easing back the breath settles the prana body. Extending furthermore, moving the body through physical stances discharges strain from your muscles.

Mental Sheath

The mental sheath comprises the fundamental working of the mind. The mind recollects, envisions, sees, and forms a sense of identity, as we talked about prior.

Memory comprises of particular storage of events from an earlier time. It's neither complete nor exact. Imagination is guess, dream, and play. It envisions what's to come, something that doesn't exist.

Sense of identity is the story about who you think you are that you have received and kept up. Accepting your story of self-esteem is as confounded as accepting that you're the utmost appearance of your body! It essentially isn't valid.

Yoga practices assist you with understanding that your story of what your identity is only a story, what's more, that you're intrinsically great. Truly, you're naturally great. Your recuperating task is to find this reality. Then you don't need to include anything extra to feel better. In your core, you're not imperfect, so there's nothing to fix and nothing to demonstrate.

Subtle Sheath (Buddhi, or Wisdom)

The following deepest sheath, the subtle sheath, or Buddhi, by and large, shows up at the point when the mind hushes up. Buddhi is additionally called the "still, little voice inside" or the "voice of internal direction." Your inward direction needs what's valid for you notwithstanding your feelings of trepidation, excruciating memories, or negative self-talk. It doesn't need for you to remain stuck in anxiety, despite the fact that your dreadful and questioning considerations may contend against its recommendation and legitimize or guard staying where you are.

Ignoring internal direction brings about more anxiety. So in spite of the fact that you might be apprehensive, putting off doing what you know, somewhere inside, you have to do essentially draws out your pressure.

Internal direction comes simpler on the off chance that you don't attempt to control, lead, or direct it. We may attempt to direct direction so as to get explicit, foreordained answers, as though we realize what's ideal and are requesting help to accomplish our objectives. At the point when we develop or endeavor to force direction, we may wind up smothering it. Requesting inward direction is an approach to look for contributions from your higher self or higher power.

While it's enticing to instruct it, requesting open-finished direction is a way to open up to genuine direction. Questions, for example, "What do I truly need to know at the present time?" and "What is life calling me to do?" assist us with getting to something more profound than the mind's gab.

Practice: Listening to Inner Guidance

1. Become aware of your body. Feel your hip bones on your seat and your feet on the floor. Feel your spine ascend out of your pelvic floor. Loosen up your shoulders. Loosen up your jaw.
2. Become aware of your energy. Notice your breath move in and out of your noses. Notice breath move into and out of your chest. Presently see breath move into and out of your stomach.
3. Request direction.
4. Spot your hand on your heart and breathe into your chest.
5. Request nondirected direction. Sit discreetly and tune in.
6. Pause. Make an opening for direction to come through. You may experience a voice, an inclination, or a knowing, or you may understand this procedure as you would a fantasy or dream. Get whatever you hear with a receptive outlook. Recording it and talking it out noisy make it more genuine for you, so compose what you hear in a diary or scratchpad and afterward tell it to somebody you trust.

Bliss Sheath

The deepest body, the bliss sheath, is the substance of what your identity is. This sheath of higher consciousness or spirituality is more testing to clarify since words can just point toward it. While this sheath can't be completely portrayed, you can identify with it, since you've encountered it.

Nothing contacts you as profoundly or mends your anxiety more profoundly than this sheath. Experiences of profound connection, harmony, and knowing, which this sheath gets to, let you know without question that you're more than your body and your mind. Most everybody has had profound experiences of higher consciousness, whether or not they were perceived accordingly. Later in this part, we reccunt stories to assist you with recalling times when you associated profoundly to live with the goal that you can reconnect to your gigantic profundity and completeness.

The Interrelationship of the Sheaths

Similarly, that yeast is gotten together with flour to make bread; the five sheaths are indistinguishable. Since they're interconnected, the physical, energy, and mental sheaths mirror the state of the others. Pain in one spreads through the others. That is the reason anxiety immerses the body, energy, and mind.

However, the higher forms of consciousness, the wisdom and bliss sheaths, don't endure; rather, they inject you with affection and truth. Go to them, become aware of them, and depend on them for your mending. Enduring happens in body, energy, and mind. Also, enduring opens you up to the domain of higher consciousness, since when you're on your knees and don't realize what else to do, you go to spiritual life. Depleted by your regular efforts to fix what is by all accounts broken, you look for comfort, understanding, and direction similarly as you're doing in perusing this book. You need help from enduring, and are going to the recuperating practices of yoga.

True Healing Involves All The Sheaths

True healing involves all the sheaths and can start in any of them.

Understanding the amazing relationship of the bodies is significant enough that we're giving another model — this time, we see how functioning with the vitality body realized healing. Since social fear, or dread of open talking, is the most across the board type of nervousness, we share Roberto's healing story.

Profound Connection

Profound connection is a type of solidarity. You can feel this profound fellowship while shaking a dozing youngster, stroking your darling pet, watching out for your garden, sitting with a perishing adored one, watching the sunrise, and a vast number of other ways. As this feeling of connection emerges, you perceive that words aren't required, that you're placated with hushing up. You feel serene what's more, absolutely without uneasiness.

Times of being "in the stream" are likewise experiences of solidarity. Whether you're running, moving, drawing, or chiseling, there's a feeling of agelessness and connectedness. You feel like nothing is wrong with the world. Nothing is missing, and life feels alright for what it's worth.

Your reasoning personality is totally submerged, with all its consideration on the present moment experience. It doesn't examine, foresee, or recall, so there's no tension.

Practice: Explore Your Profound Connection

Experiences

Recollect times of profound connection and experiences of being "in the flow." Tell your experiences to somebody you trust or compose about them in a diary. Give yourself a chance to be moved by recalling, composing, and telling. Rediscover what you're inflexibly associated with life.

Near-Death Experiences

Other amazing occasions of higher cognizance, for example, near-death experiences, can modify your feeling of what your identity is and what makes a difference to you. Near-death experiences, whether or not they're emotional, help you to remember your mortality. Following is a near-death experience that incredibly affected Rick.

We're sharing it here to stir your memory.

Spiritual Opening

A spiritual opening is an occasion or arrangement of occasions that answers the inquiry, "who am I?" An encounter of raised awareness it gives you who you genuinely are. It moves your point of view so as to not decipher life from the restricted point of view of your adapted personality. Subsequently, you experience all of life as sacrosanct.

Regardless you live in your body and have your brain with all its accounts. An old story may pull at you, even hurl you around somewhat, yet then, inexplicably, you see it, call it by its name, and grin at it. You understand that your old stories are the functions of a kid's brain. As a mother, you look over to perceive what your kid's psyche is doing and afterward divert your consideration back to the present. You go to the favored stillness for direction as opposed to letting old stories settle on significant choices. You tap into the inhabiting spot of calm and bliss, not simply because it feels superb, but since you realize that it generally will be your true self and your true home.

Spiritual openings happen in close to nothing and large ways. There's one key acknowledgment, whether it's a passing acknowledgment or an enduring movement of awareness.

Any snapshot of acknowledgment that you're mindfulness, cognizance, or soul changes your feeling of what your identity is. It's simply that you may overlook, yet luckily you can recall once more.

Stephanie's Dream

God was in my mind, giving me scenes from my adolescence and conversing with me, in my very own voice. Huge numbers of the scenes were horrible. A portion of the scenes were of grown-ups being caring to me. In each scene, God stated, "I was there with you." The dream finished with God saying, again in my voice, "I am with you generally; I will never spurn you." Stephanie included that in spite of the fact that she'd had the dream numerous years prior, it still intensely affected her. Then she said in a quieted voice, "There's no uncertainty that I'm a cognizant being, that I'm adored, that I'm rarely alone.

Practice: Your Precious Self

What minutes, dreams, and experiences left you with the mindfulness that you're a sign of cognizance or a son of God? How could they modify your feeling of character? Maybe you heard a tune or read a petition and realized you were a hallowed being, maybe you felt a caring nearness with you, or perhaps you had a genuine sickness that left you with most likely that you're more than your impermanent body and brain. Advise your experiences to somebody you trust or expound on them. Give yourself a chance to recollect once more.

Conclusion

The move from tension to happiness happens when sympathy, understanding, and profound connection penetrate the body, brain, and vitality. True healing incorporates all five sheaths. Yoga rehearses intended to make you aware of not just your external layer yet additionally your deepest self. This section urged you to reconnect with your pith. As you proceed with your adventure of healing, recollect who you genuinely are. To develop your understanding of nervousness, we currently move to an investigation of the basic reasons for tension.

CHAPTER 4: A DEEPER LOOK AT ANXIETY

When you enter into your suffering, a lot of the suffering is relieved.

—Father Basil Pennington

At the point when you venture into the spots of anxiety, you don't need to enter alone. You have to breathe to unfaltering you and seeing to hold your hand. With these partners, you don't get lost. Bolstered, you can see, feel, and comprehend in ways that soothe your affliction. With the goal that you can enter your places of anxiety, we look next at kleshas, which is Sanskrit for "burdens." Considered to be the essential drivers of human misery, there are five distresses, all of which can lead to anxiety. As we discuss them, we welcome you to ask into potential ways they add to your anxiety.

Ignorance (Avidya)

Ignorance—just "not knowing" (in Sanskrit, avidya)—is a principal reason for misery. Everybody has encountered the agonizing results of deciding in view of missing or deficient data. In the outcome of such decisions, you shake your head and whisper,"I wish I had known."Decisions dependent on misunderstanding cause enduring. The best ignorance of all is mistaking the incredible for the genuine, that is, the point at which you can't distinguish your self-constraining story from the more profound truth of what your identity is. Human life is miraculous. You've without a doubt been awed by the guiltless magnificence of newborn children, detecting that they're a cherished endowment of life. Incredibly, you may disregard that your life is similarly as miraculous. Nearly all of us fall under the spell of spiritual ignorance and overlook what our identity is. At the point when the information that you are holy slips into obviousness, all that is left is the everyday. Your sense of what your identity is diminished to considerations, thoughts, body parts, and things, which are consistently changing and momentary, and you definitely feel, by one way or another, inadequate and discontented. You need to look for bliss, since you don't encounter it in yourself.

Not detecting your spiritual quintessence, you have no place of refuge, no inward spot of comfort. At the point when you don't have the foggiest idea about what you are soul or awareness, profound inside, you feel an existential aloneness that causes enormous anxiety. What's more, when you do detect your pith, you feel satisfied and upbeat for reasons unknown.

Not knowing what your identity makes you experience yourself as deprived of the spiritual, as it did Ben.

Work on: Exploring Ignorance

Here are inquiries to control you in investigating ignorance. Give yourself a lot of time to reply so you'll be conveyed past shallow answers into an all the more noteworthy investigation.

> - How does my physical body decide my feeling of self-worth?
> - How does my appearance influence my anxiety?
> - How does my status in external life decide my feeling of self?
> - How does my status influence my anxiety?
> - How is my feeling of self affected when I "come up short" or "succeed"?
> - When do I most experience the holy?
> - When would I be able to give myself calm time to revive and reflect?

Expound on an encounter that was spiritually nourishing.

Limited Self-Concept (Asmita)

Limited self-concept (or in Sanskit, *asmita*) is when we mistakenly believe the self-limiting stories we tell ourselves: "I'm an anxious person," "I'm an angry person, "I'm a sad person," and so on. This form of suffering is caused by not challenging the old ideas and stories you tell yourself. You know that you're in the grips of limited self-concept when you hear yourself say, "I've always been like this; I can't change. This is just the way I am."Asmita is the seal of "innocent misunderstanding," believing the old story of identity.

Work on: Breaking Free

To break free from your historical feeling of self, affectionately go up against your restricting convictions. Return to the constraining convictions you hovered in the past training. With the thoughtfulness of a caring grandmother, inquire yourself the accompanying inquiries:

> ➤ "How long have I been stating this?"
> ➤ "Is this conviction really true?"

➢ "Do I know without a doubt this is true?"
➢ "What does the information state?"

Basically, posing the inquiries brings mindfulness. You don't need to reframe the story, make up a superior story, or fix it in any capacity. By basically getting mindful of the story, you let go of its oblivious impact over you.

Here's a case of how one lady in her mid-thirties challenged a story she had continued from adolescence into adulthood.

Attachment (raga)

Another klesha is attachment, or raga, which is the frightful clutching something pleasurable or wanted. The vitality of attachment resembles a hand that sticks and handles into a tight fist. Attachment isn't about "who" you think you are; rather, it's about what you think you need so as to be alright. It's the sense that you must have a specific something to make your life alright. At the point when you hear yourself state, "I must have," "I'd kick the bucket without," or "It needs to be, "you're in the holds of attachment.

Attachment has an unmistakable clingy enthusiastic nature of earnestness. The enthusiastic charge is solid. Attachment is not simply thinking something; it's sticking urgently to something. Attachments are very much characterized, explicit: "I need this relationship," "I need this sort of occupation," "I have to know."

The Brain and Attachment

In his book Light on The Yoga Sūtras of Patañjali, B. K. S. Iyengar (1993) composed that attachment is related to the nerve center in the brain. This almond-molded gland, found profound inside the brain, controls some substantial functions, including pulse, pulse, and internal heat level, and is an organizer of the autonomic sensory system. Profoundly delicate to emotional stress, the nerve center responds to dangers, genuine or envisioned, by conveying hormonal messages. This procedure, which triggers the battle or-flight response, sidesteps the coherent, thinking part about the brain.

Attachment, being related to the nerve center, sidesteps reason. Presently you can value the strong emotional charge attachment has. Attachment is so ground-breaking that in the book Yoga and Psychotherapy (Swami Rama, Ballentine, and Ajaya 1976), Swami Rama alludes to it as the essential driver of anxiety.

Attachment to Certainty and Control

At the point when you stress over and are distracted with the future, you need certainty since you're attempting to make sense of what will occur in the future with the goal that you can be set up for it and therefore be in control. Additionally, at the point when you cinch down on your emotions, you apply incredible exertion to be in control of yourself. You don't have any desire to seem frail, feel defenseless, or experience undesirable emotions, so you attempt to keep yourself in your security zone.

Being careful and secure is an endurance response, however feeling that you have to seem strong and safe continuously is another thing.

How about we take a gander at fears and how they relate to attachment to certainty. A fear is an irrational, extreme, and persistent dread of some specific thing or situation. An irrational dread of lifts, flying in planes, open talking, driving alone when street conditions are protected, and so on incredibly constrains you when you allow it to be an essential main impetus in your decision making. It's one thing to have such a dread and another to give it a chance to control your lifestyle, which it does when you should be in control of your emotions makes you avoid doing exercises you may otherwise appreciate and discover valuable.

Nearly everyone is joined to control and certainty at some level. True healing from anxiety involves seeing and recognizing our fundamental attachment to control and certainty. We should apply this to recuperation from trauma, since trauma is an incessant reason for anxiety as well as is experienced by the vast majority eventually in their lives.

The result of trauma unavoidably incorporates a development toward control and certainty. How would it be able to not? On the off chance that we've slipped on the stairs and hurt ourselves, we arrange those stairs all the more cautiously later on. On the off chance that we've been severely harmed in a fender bender, we might be increasingly cautious later on when we drive. On the off chance that someone in our lives has sold out us, we may abstain from having anything to do with that person later on. Trauma, by its tendency, breaks our feeling of security. In the same way that a creature goes to its cave to recuperate, you retreat to whatever puts inside yourself, just as in the external world, feel the most secure to you.

In like manner, after physical damage, it's therapeutic to strengthen your physical body through rest, great nutrition, and exercise. In consequence of emotional wounds, it's healing to create limits with individuals, thoughts, and situations that are hurtful to you. The two procedures are essential for your recuperation and assist you with reconstructing your feeling of wellbeing. Be that as it may, healing doesn't end there; it additionally incorporates figuring out how to endure uncertainty, in light of the fact that as we as a whole know, life offers no assurances of constant wellbeing and security. Healing involves getting ready to manage the unavoidable anxiety that goes with proceeding onward and keeping our hearts open. As you read on, you'll find numerous particular approaches to assist you with managing exceptional dread and anxiety, for example, the solace posture to diminish emotional upset

Absence of Attachment

To understand this all the more altogether, how about we take a gander at the absence of attachment, or then again nonattachment, which involves living contentedly with uncertainty. As you know, life's not static; it changes and moves. The absence of attachment is tolerating life for what it's worth.

It's not all that simple to do! Our brains withdraw from giving up and giving life a chance to be as it is. We don't have any desire to recognize that our thoughts regarding how we think life ought to contribute to our pressure. (Incidentally, that is no joke looking for control; this reflex is an extension of the endurance nature of protection. A few would state it's essentially your conscience carrying out its responsibility, endeavoring to ensure you.) Yet it's healing to recognize that you unavoidably think and feel that life ought to be other than it is. Essentially conceding your craving for control discharges its hold on you and encourages you manage life, especially with things you wish weren't going on.

Tolerating "what is" is the core of nonattachment, and incorporates perceiving what's going on within you just as what's going on in the external world. Tolerating "what is" incorporates all your considerations and emotional reactions to occasions that happen around you. Acknowledgment doesn't really mean affirming or loving; it suggests perceiving what's actually happening and figuring out how to live all the more easily with life all things considered. Nor does it mean uninvolved noninvolvement. In truth, you settle on enabled decisions when you're mindful of what's happening. For model, recognizing that you're figuring, I don't care for what's going on; I'm scared, and then taking a full breath or two so you don't lose all sense of direction in your emotions, encourages you to evaluate whether or not there's anything you can do about the situation.

Denying "what is" is something contrary to nonattachment. Disavowal is the most ground-breaking mental guard mechanism, so how about we give it our due regard.

Tolerating things that occur, how you feel, and what you believe are no small errands. And yet, true healing asks you to, and you can, with the assistance of your companions, breathing and seeing, and numerous other yoga rehearses.

Taking part in meditation, request, devotional supplication, and mantra (recounting a wise or hallowed word or expression), just as perusing your preferred holy sacred writings, causes you to acknowledge life for what it's worth. These practices connect you with higher consciousness so you can say, "Let proceed to let God," or some other expression that interests to you, and ride the influx of your restless sentiments. Breathing and seeing, you can give such sentiments a chance to travel through you without them retraumatizing you.

Janette's healing story shows the intensity of nonattachment in recouping from emotional and physical trauma.

Attachment to Being Perfect

Perfectionism is a power that tramples compassion and squelches satisfaction. A tenacious weight, perfectionist thinking hasn't the faintest idea about your intrinsic worth, so it gives you severe rules about how to make yourself into an adequate someone. No wonder it's firmly connected to anxiety. On the off chance that you endure from needing to be perfect, you have repeating contemplations about observing principles, meeting elevated requirements; and strengthening unbending, moralistic standards. With perfectionism as a main impetus in your life, you may accept that you can win and strengthen your self-worth by following severe rules and accomplishing very explicit outcomes. As you read on, consider whether you have propensities toward perfectionism. You may have a couple of the qualities or experience the ill effects of progressively inescapable perfectionism. Either way, it might contribute to your anxiety.

In Too Perfect, Allan E. Mallinger and Jeannette DeWyze (1992) clarify that perfectionists need to feel in control consistently to have a sense of security. They dread shading outside the lines and make a solid effort to consent to self-forced standards, frequently ones they don't completely understand. Through carefulness and extraordinary exertion, perfectionists endeavor to hit the nail on the head. Would you be able to detect the tension this makes? This tension, which is shared by such huge numbers of us, can be deadening, making us reluctant to endeavor whatever we or others may pass judgment.

Perfectionism And Addiction

In the event that you experience the ill effects of perfectionism, you might be dependent on work, having a perfect body, or being a perfect person. These addictions uncover the internal strain to "hit the nail on the head." The compulsive worker centers around work efficiency or greatness. The perfect-body someone who is addicted looks for a set bodyweight and attire size.

And the perfect-person someone who is addicted forces unbending good and social codes. Meeting the standards overshadows everything else, including getting a charge out of life and relationships with others. The critical strain to be perfect and the subsequent isolation can cause high and chronic anxiety—and cause you to be less and less mindful of your consecrated quintessence.

Perfectionism And Criticism

In case you're perfectionistic, you're most likely both exceptionally touchy to criticism and disparaging of others. Truth be told, the hallmark of perfectionism is basic.

Censuring yourself feels natural, even accommodating, as an inspiration to improve.

Hearing criticism from others, however, can take advantage of your fundamental conviction that you're defective. Criticism feels disgracing and incapacitating, which stops you in your tracks and keeps you from attempting new things, doing anything inventive, or going for broke. A few perfectionists are latent and do all that they can to be invisible, to abstain from being seen or having attention attracted to them. Others, in view of their faultless appearance and execution, may look great to others. In spite of the fact that perfectionism is difficult and causes high anxiety, other individuals may not see the perfectionist's anguish. Outwardly, it might look as if you're profoundly spurred and in control.

Aversion (Dvesa)

Aversion (in Sanskrit, dvesa) is the other side of attachment. For each attachment, there's an aversion; for all that you stick to, there's something from which you withdraw. Aversion is the motivation to dodge or move away from something, whether it's a person, movement, item, or thought. You're in the grasps of aversion when you state, "I can't hold up under this," "I couldn't in any way, shape or form manage it," "I can't stand such and such," or "I have a debilitated inclination at sight or thought of this."Associated with the nerve center similarly that attachment is, aversion is an amazing vitality that triggers a sentiment of danger or extreme weakness when you're not actually looked with a fast-approaching risk to your wellbeing. Obviously, you naturally move away from something that is really potentially destructive, for example, driving the wrong route on a one-path street during heavy traffic, starting the moment you see oncoming traffic until you get yourself and your vehicle off the street or securely convoluted.

Like attachment, aversion is a fortifying arrangement of reactions between speculation and the body's pressure response. Thusly, it can turn into an endless loop. The nerve center triggers the body's battle or-flight response dependent on the brain's saying, I can't bear. The mind then judges the physical discomfort as deplorable, which thusly raises the pressure response.

Feel it yourself, in the event that you like. Only for a minute, envision that something's happening that you're disinclined to, for example, giving an open presentation or being told your zipper's down. In the event that the idea of these things happening triggers even a gentle aversion, see how your body fires up only a bit. Your heart pulsates a little harder, and you may squirm.

This is only an exercise. What you fear isn't actually occurring; however, you are envisioning it in your brain. However, in any event, contemplating it or recalling horrendous pictures causes the pressure response. This awkward exercise shows how aversion is made. Aversion is something that you figure you can't hold up under or that you know could compromise your prosperity in the event that it actually occurred. One of the more anxiety-delivering aversions is the idea of living on after someone dear to you passes on. The vast majority pull back from this notion. It appears agonizing. In any event, considering the plausibility causes agony, setting off an aversion to discussing it, seeing a film about it, finding out about it, or in any event, heading off to a companion's memorial service.

Fear of Loving

Fear of death is often changed into a fear of loving. Psychologically, the fear of loving again after someone near you has kicked the bucket is an aversion. You may figure you can't stand to give up and love again, realizing that you'll risk losing someone again and lamenting all over once more. It's our human nature to adore. Love is widespread and knows no limits; it's only the human personality that makes limitations around affection. To believe that we can love only one person, pet, article, lifestyle, or period of life is a misunderstanding of the manner in which life is. We don't realize to what extent we'll live, or to what extent those we love will be with us or love us consequently. Truth be told, understanding that we are all only on earth for some time causes us to prize our friends and family and keep from taking them for conceded. The greater part of us fall shy of loving others or ourselves so straightforwardly, so the genuine healing move is to grasp everything, even our keeping down from adoration compassionately.

Misfortunes, for example, death, separation, disability, and disaster, aren't anything but difficult to bargain with, nor is relinquishing youth and material accomplishment in a culture that worships both. Misfortune harms. It requires some investment to mend and acknowledge your affliction. Profound sadness is an incredible vitality that initially feels persevering and then later comes in waves. Metaphorically, and once in a while, literally, it can drop you to your knees. To state that you'll never adore again because of the torment of melancholy is heartbreaking due to the self-limitations it gets underway. In the event that you've lost a pet, you know this personally. The melancholy that goes with the death of an adored creature can be extraordinary. The only path through the sorrow is to give yourself a chance to feel it, realizing that misery is a part of adoration. Through its expression, your heart stays open, empowering you to bond with another creature.

Along these lines, individuals move in and out of your life. Saying, "I don't know whether I can adore again, "during the early periods of misery gives you an opportunity to grieve. Be that as it may, in the long take, saying, "I'll never love again on the grounds that endings hurt excessively," cuts you off from life and your loving nature.

Fear of Abandonment

As a part of the fear of death, we need to address a more subtle, however very ground-breaking fear. The fear of abandonment is a mental fear that appears to be connected to physical endurance. You hear this fear in expressions, for example, "I feel that I would bite the dust on the off chance that he left me," "I can't make it on my own," "I need her," and "I can't be alone." Hidden this fear is the conviction that you're only alright, or safe when you clutch what you by and by have. While it's straightforward the instinctual requirement for physical security, here we're discussing mental wellbeing. This difficult fear confuses emotional help from a particular person with physical endurance itself.

How about we include somewhat viewpoint. It's not unexpected to have reliance needs, sound to depend on friends and family for emotional help, and common to frame close bonds with others. It's not unordinary to have some fear of being abandoned. Fear of abandonment goes beyond typical grown-up human interdependency. At its underlying foundations, this is a profound conviction that you can't make due on your own, without the help of this other person. Subsequently, you may fear desertion or selling out and maybe indeed, even observe indications of rejection where there are none. This can likewise appear as fear of closeness, coming from the conviction that the ideal approach to anticipate your experience of abandonment is to abstain from getting excessively close in any case.

We should be compassionate as we investigate this fear. Endless individuals endure from fear of abandonment in differing degrees. This fear often originates from recollections of youth experiences of being abandoned or ignored, physically or then again emotionally. Abandonment in adolescence can have long-enduring impacts, since kids need a guardian's protection, love, and consolation. Without a physical safe house, youngsters become feeble; without emotional help, kids' emotional advancement withers, and without contact, small newborn children usually pass away. In the event that your anxiety appears as the fear of abandonment, your expectation for recuperation rests in perceiving what's happening. In the event that you have this fear, you may perceive a portion of the accompanying: anxiety even at the idea of being alone, turning out to be on edge except if you get constant consolation, connecting for closeness improperly, suspecting selling out without proof that it's happening, freezing over small indiscretions, enjoying emotional extortion that can be communicated as "I'll hurt myself in the event that you leave," or a blend of these. In the event that you become mindful of the structure your anxiety is taking, you'll never again unconsciously be held hostage by the spell of this excruciating fear. In the event that your anxiety takes any of these structures, realize that you're not alone. In the event that fear of abandonment is extraordinary, you may profit by professional guiding. Additionally, you can help yourself with yoga rehearses.

Recognizing Fear of Abandonment

Be delicate in recognizing this fear. See it, face it, and take a gander at it. Keep in mind, getting conscious of it is the initial move toward freedom from anxiety. Give yourself some credit. While the help of others is vital, they're not constantly accessible to you. Be that as it may, you're constantly accessible to you, and you can figure out how to be strong of yourself. You don't need to abandon yourself. As a starter, breathe profoundly and whisper, "I am here, for myself; I am here."

As you experience this book, give the practices a shot and sense which ones work for you. Investigate how you could personalize them to make them feel perfect for you. Then guarantee your individualized yoga practice as your own, realizing that you can alter it when you need to. Go to your practices and depend on them, and they'll not just become as dear as a believed companion; however, will likewise give abilities that see you through your tempests.

Conclusion

There are five causes of suffering:

1. Ignorance of truth
2. Limited self-concept
3. Attachment
4. Aversion
5. Fear of death

It's useful to take a gander at them independently with the goal that you can perceive how the underlying drivers of anxiety live in you. Notwithstanding, they're all interrelated and mutually impact one another. Attachment, an incredible reason for anxiety, results from our endeavors to clutch what we think we need so as to feel OK. It's identified with ignorance, since when we don't know what our identity is, we must have something to stick to so as to feel enabled. Since you have some sense about the hidden reasons for anxiety and how it lives in you, it's an ideal opportunity to dive all the more profoundly into the yoga rehearses that quiet your on edge mind.

CHAPTER 5: PRACTICES FOR CALMING YOUR MIND

Human beings, when not stressed, are utterly beautiful. It's only when we are confused that our hearts shrivel, and our minds figure crafty ways out of situations…. When we relate to life from our minds, we take our feet off the ground. It's like not wanting to touch the floor, fearing that we will be burned. — Stephen Levine

Our minds do as well as can be expected as they attempt to ensure us and assist us with navigating as the days progressed. The mind hasn't the faintest idea that it keeps us frightful and troubled, yet it does. In this part, we make you stride by step through practices that engage you to put your on edge considerations to rest and stir your ability to satisfy your most genuine wants. You don't need to remain an innocent casualty of uneasiness producing considerations. You can shape your life by using your inner direction and your loving heart as you figure out how to take advantage of them and tail them where they take you. Since dread producing considerations frequently fly underneath the radar screen of our mindfulness, we don't realize they're influencing us. All things considered, they are, and here's an amazing guarantee. Not exclusively would you be able to get mindful of your contemplations, in any case, you can likewise truly fill your mind with contemplations that will assist you with actualizing your human potential. Truth be told, the guarantee of this section doesn't only help from nervousness yet additionally the solace and satisfaction that originate from being completely alive while keeping your feet on the ground.

Becoming Conscious In The Present Moment

We should begin with the conspicuous that isn't so self-evident. The entirety of life, including the encounters of nervousness and delight, happens in the present moment. You envision the future in the present moment, which is what you're doing when you stew about something that hasn't yet occurred. In the present moment, you wring your hands over what may occur. For the most part, the entirety of your experience feels genuine, regardless of whether it's absolutely random to what's really happening in the physical reality outside of you.

Suppose you're settled in your bed and dozing off to rest at 10:30 p.m., at the point when the phone rings. You wonder if something's wrong, and your heart skirts a beat as you reach toward the end table to pick up the phone. Anxious, you answer, and it's a wrong number. Alleviated that it's not awful news, you hang up what's more; twist back up in your bed. Your dread wasn't brought about by the phone's ringing; it was brought about by your internal response to it.

In case you're similar to the vast majority, it might appear as though you have no control over such fears, that they simply wash over you. You can figure out how to be increasingly mindful of your dreadful and troubling contemplations from moment to moment, and figure out how to identify with your tension, and even decrease it, so you can manage things that as a matter of fact occur. At the point when you stress, you're somewhere out in dreamland and looted of the probability of focusing on what you truly need or on constructive issue solving.

Imprints On The Mind (Samskaras)

Recurring musings, thoughts, and practices cut profoundly ingrained trenches or sections into our minds. Called samskaras in the Yoga tradition, these imprints have a strong gravitational destroy that can be hard to oppose after some time. Samskaras can affect your life, for example, when you have sound propensities, or they can be damaging, for example, when you rehash foolish practices that keep you caught in a painful groove. Samskaras are shaped through repetition. Each time you rehash an idea or copy a conduct, you cut all the more profoundly into its notch in your mind, reinforcing it as a propensity (Forbes 2004, 2008). Each troubling idea about whether or not someone prefers you scratches into the apprehension indentation Imagine a scenario where individuals don't care for me. As the section gets further, it turns into a more amazing power that prompts future actions or, for this situation, more stresses. In other words, your contemplations and practices mark your mind as well as combine as impressions that lead to future actions.

As Georg Feuerstein states in The Yoga Tradition (1998, 320), samskaras live in your subconscious as "subliminal activators" that shape your contemplations, feelings, and actions on the planet. As you can detect, they have gigantic control over you; they even determine the conditions of your future life, if you let them continue to take a shot at you subconsciously. Your old center stories are solidly settled in samskaras; so are old injury recollections and constant troubling contemplations. Luckily, the impact of becoming mindful of them, when they emerge, is similarly amazing. Distinguish and witness your old stories, and over time, your scores smooth out, which liberates you from repeating reckless propensities. Neuroscience is verifying the yogic perspective on the mind's samskaras. In mind and the Brain (2002), Jeffrey Schwartz and

Sharon Begley detailed that researchers have discovered that the action of rehashed firings of neurons changes the wiring of the brain. This implies you can change your psychological wiring by what you think and how frequently you think it. Rehashed on edge, contemplations burrow profound grooves. Give them a chance to flee with you, and they make trenches that are difficult to get out of. Luckily, calming and encouraging contemplations additionally cut tracks into your brain, developing your ability to be more quiet, in any event, when you experience life's unpleasant spots.

Prior to proceeding, we need to point out that we've improved the procedure of how examples are framed in the brain so you can work with your own "design making." in the event that what we're saying sounds robotic, we need to include that the procedure involves a phenomenal cooperative energy of actually billions of brain cells firing and forming associations with one another. Science can't completely explain what occurs, in light of the fact that while your brain's electrical activity can be estimated, the particular action can't be estimated. How the procedure happens remains a secret, yet we can get conscious of what we think and how those considerations influence us.

On the off chance that you remain unconscious of your contemplations, then you're helpless before powers that Rick calls "attractive tracks in mind." When you become mindful of contemplations that keep you stuck or cause you nervousness, you can interrupt them and mitigate your misery. Consider how alleviated you'll feel when you can get your samskara in a sentence and respond, "Here I am, concerned again that I'll fail." Doing so naturally makes you respite and take a breath, which interrupts the idea, giving you a moment to regroup and an opportunity to change your course. Later in this part, you'll figure out how to substitute empowering musings that structure sound scores in your mind; for example, Here I am. I can breathe and center, and put forth a valiant effort. Not exclusively do you then make soundtracks in your mind; however, you likewise let the old ones that reason to such an extent, pain become torpid. Be delicate as you approach your samskaras. In the event that you will, in general, be reproachful of yourself, samskaras can become something else that is wrong with me, and you may utilize them as weapons against yourself. Beating up on you doesn't mitigate nervousness. Everyone has samskaric inclinations. Despite the fact that your suffering is personal to you, your samskaras aren't interesting, and you're not alone in your inclinations. For the time being, the point at which you hear old news, calmly inhale and murmur to yourself, "Samskara—old innocent misunderstanding."

Becoming Aware

To become aware of samskaras, first we have to understand what we mean by becoming aware. Being aware intends to learn, to recognize, or to be alert. Awareness doesn't deliver understanding; it seeks understanding. Unbiased and calm, without commenting, awareness basically gives you what's going on.

Becoming aware of samskaras enables you, in light of the fact that once something registers in your consciousness, you respond to it in an unexpected way, for example, when you find a trench in the street and delayed down or drive around it. Along these lines, being capable to soothe tension and find comfort in your physical body relies upon your becoming aware of what's going on. During a scene of uplifted nervousness, your awareness centers around the distress you feel. You're enveloped with an encounter of stress and dread, and don't realize that you're unconsciously creating it yourself. Everything necessary, however, is something else to redirect your attention, and troubling considerations stop. For model, suppose you're apprehensive about something, and then the doorbell rings, diverting your attention. You stroll to the entryway and welcome your neighbor. You take part in a brief conversation about the local excursion and, for a couple minutes, have no uneasiness. After the neighbor leaves, your attention returns to your concern, and you again experience uneasiness. This model gives you that at the point when you become aware of something other than your troubling contemplations, your nervousness stops. You don't need to hang tight for something else to interrupt your stress; you can become aware of what you're thinking and interrupt it yourself by directing your awareness to something soothing, for example, your breath; a kind thought like Hush, my dear; or noticing hues in the room around you.

The Capacity to Direct Awareness

You can figure out how to direct your awareness. For instance, you direct awareness away from considerations and into action when you state to yourself, "Enough worrying; focus on doing the dishes." You can move awareness from musings to sensations to emotions. You can move it from inside you to outside of you, from a limited to a wide horizon, and from grosser to increasingly unobtrusive stimulation. The most straightforward approach to understand this is to encounter it firsthand.

Helping Yourself

You can utilize the capacity to move awareness to support yourself. Knowing that stress doesn't soothe you, when you find that you're worrying, move your concentrate somewhere else. Offer your stressed mind a reprieve by letting your musings be without paying attention to them. Put some space between your attention and your troubling musings. Check out your general surroundings. Utilize your faculties: tune in, see, smell, taste, and touch. Become conscious of what's happening around you. This actually brings you to your faculties and makes you aware of life in the present moment.

On the off chance that you feel the hints of nervousness or the destroy of samskaras trying to take you once more into distress, decide to concentrate on something pleasing. Tune in to a song, look at a tree, smell the natural air, drink a glass of water, or back rub your lower arms. Plan something to invigorate and restore yourself, and then go on about your day or address whatever you have to confront.

Become Aware Of What Soothes And Calms

Your awareness inclines toward strong stimulation, which is the reason you take note uproarious sounds more than calm ones. Imagine that you have a pigeon cooing on one shoulder and a parrot squawking on the other. You'll make some hard memories focusing on the sound of the bird, since its cooing is muffled by the higher pitch and volume of the parrot. You wind up, reacting to the parrot, and the soothing coos of the bird go unnoticed. In your mind, dreadful considerations are as uproarious as a squawking parrot, and soothing considerations are often as calm as a cooing dove. It's hard to dislodge your awareness from strong stimulation, whether it's a parrot or dreadful considerations. A parrot doesn't stop screeching since you aren't paying attention to it, and neither do noisy, dreadful musings. Nervousness can be profoundly stimulating, and attempting to redirect your attention away from it by focusing on soothing contemplations or something comforting in your environment might be ineffective now and again. Next, we give interventions to direct and intense distress. The two interventions involve moving your physical body or doing something that feels great to your physical body. They consist of shifting your awareness from mental and emotional pain to physical delight, which, of course, you must know about as it happens in the present moment.

Move Your Physical Body to Dislodge Awareness from Distress

In case you're respectably fomented, it might take moderate stimulation to occupy your attention. You may need to accomplish something dynamic, for example, take a warm shower, walk the pooch, or move to your preferred music. On the off chance that you have less time or aren't at home, find something else to take your attention off your nervousness. Go to the washroom and wash your face; say, "Ahhhhh, ahhhh," boisterously two or three times; stand up and stretch; or stroll over to a window and look outside. You don't need to endure interminably; however, you do need to recognize what to do to help yourself and then really do it. Indeed, even a thirty-second break can make a tremendous distinction.

Now and then, strong distress requires a similarly strong diversion. At the point when you're totally adjacent to yourself, attempt thoroughly moving your body. It might snap you out of a tension stupor or bob you up out of a profound samskaric groove. In any case, whatever you do, know about what you're doing, so it's not mindless movement. we give you explicit yoga presents you can do as a training to alleviate uneasiness. For the time being, we'll train a movement intervention to shake awareness free from uneasiness.

CHAPTER 6: PRACTICES FOR COMFORTING YOUR BODY

Your life becomes a temple of that which is sacred when you choose to live with love in this moment. — Swami Chetanananda

It's alongside difficult to know about the nearness of the hallowed when your heart is deterred, and nervousness and injury make you need to close down on occasion, disconnect from your loving nature. Your healing relies upon your opening up again and remaining open. It's additionally hard to encounter your life as heavenly when your body is tight, regularly bracing against conceivable risk. Whether or not you're aware of it, tension negatively affects your body and your heart. One of the most secure, best approaches to open your heart and solace your body is with an ordinary, delicate act of yoga presents.

Once your body and your breath have been immersed with dread, they commonly reinforce your distress and propagate uneasiness. As a result of their nearby relationship, when you practice yoga represents, it's imperative to likewise concentrate on your breathing. You stretch, move, and hold presents while being aware of your breath.

The speculative chemistry of doing so causes your training to transformational and more than simply physical exercise. Luckily, you don't need to be physically fit to rehearse and advantage from yoga for nervousness. A carefully chosen act of charming yoga represents that are within your physical capacity helps clear the impacts of nervousness out of your body and heart, particularly on the off chance that you practice them all the time. Taking ten to fifteen minutes every day to do a couple of stances keeps your body free of stored-up nervousness in the equivalent way that customary brushing keeps your teeth and gums free of microscopic organisms. The postures we educate in the following pages are protected, feel better, and restore a feeling of solace to your body. The stances are for use as vital, for those occasions when you're overpowered or need additional solace. We instruct five simple stances you can do day by day, and we've included five additional stances you can take into your everyday practice when you possess energy for a longer practice. Then we conclude with a couple of yogic breathing practices since learning to breathe completely is so therapeutic.

How you practice these yoga presents relies upon the kind of person you are and how you experience uneasiness. To assist you with selecting an approach to rehearse that truly suits you, here's a little information about what other individuals have found. John Kabat-Zinn, author of the Stress Reduction Clinic at the University of Massachusetts Medical School, and associates (Kabat-Zinn, Chapman, and Salmon 1997) found that individuals who experience nervousness more as mental distress will, in general, prefer to move and strengthen their bodies in their training, and the individuals who feel uneasiness more as distress in the body incline toward a calmer, less physical, thoughtful methodology. In this way, in case you're a worrier, you may need begin your training with represents that warmth your body, for example, the scaffold present stream (where you move into and out of the represent a few times), or the muscle-strengthening presents, such as vessel and staff, for some time and then step by step include propelled variations of stances to your training. In the event that your body feels trembly and you're vexed, attempt a delicate practice, for example, the five simple stances; do two or three minutes of substitute nostril breathing, and then sit in meditation. These postures and breathing strategies are introduced later in this section. Judith Lasater (1995), an authority in restorative yoga, found that during times of exhaustion, individual's advantage most from upheld represents that they rest in for a few minutes. In these stances, you prop up your body with covers, cushions, and yoga squares (yoga props roughly the size of two thick books) so that you feel upheld and don't strain.

Restorative postures have a sense of security and emotionally stabilizing while delicately allowing your body to open and unwind. In case you're exhausted from later or ongoing injury, the restorative posture for emotional weakness might be therapeutic for you and might be the only present you practice until you have the capacity for doing the five simple stances.

Doing yoga stances to lessen tension bodes well. They're relaxing, calm, strong tension, and strengthen muscles. In any case, the advantages expand a long ways beyond the physical. They give you a fundamental feeling of having a strong foundation, help you to absorb your encounters, and engage you to live with an open heart. To explain these underlying advantages, how about we take a gander at vitality centers.

Psychoenergetic Centers (Chakras)

Similarly, that ground-breaking flows travel through the sea, vitality continuously moves through your body and mind. In spite of the fact that vitality goes in numerous directions in our bodies, and especially strong current moves along the spine. There are additionally vitality centers, called **chakras**, along the spine. Three are underneath the heart, and three are above it.

Vitality can become caught within these centers. One approach to get a feeling of caught vitality is to contrast it with strong tension. Muscles are intended to contract when required and loosen up when not being utilized. At the point when muscles are tense, they remain contracted, which you experience as fits, solidness, and inconvenience. At the point when your muscles unwind, you feel great in your body.

Essentially, caught vitality in your chakra centers impacts you drastically.

Maybe most clear is what happens when your heart chakra is cut off, which makes you feel wanton, indifferent, or even untouched by suffering and delight. At the point when your heart chakra is open, you feel inviting, responsive, and warm.

Like water flowing down the Mississippi River into the Gulf of Mexico, it's ideal to have vitality flowing openly all through your body. Tension disturbs this stream by causing tension and agitation. The three chakras that most directly pertain to anxiety are the root support (muladhara), jewel fortress (manipura), and unstuck (anahata).

Yoga poses for anxiety focus on these three energy centers.

Root Support (Muladhara) Chakra

The first and last chakra, muladhara, is situated at the base of the spine at the perineal floor. The Sanskrit word muladhara signifies "root support." This focus reflects essential endurance issues. As indicated by Gary Kraftsow in Yoga for Change (2002), this chakra identifies with your hips, knees, and feet. Found at the base of the spine, this chakra speaks to strength. As you surely understand, when you and your life are steady, you're increasingly well-suited to feel more secure and think that it's simpler to trust, and when things are precarious, you may feel increasingly frightful and doubting. Injury relates to endurance, since it upsets your feeling of security.

Vivaciously put away in the most reduced chakra, injury causes strain in the hips.

At first, while experiencing a harsh time, you normally fix and secure yourself. Be that as it may, to remain shut is awful. There comes an opportunity to open, to be open to life once more, else you're immobilized and impaired. Yoga represents that discharge put away pressure in the hips are restorative for anxiety, since they open and loosen up the body tissue around the hip zone. Forward folding presents, for example, what you do when you plunk down and twist around to tie your shoes, are successful at discharging pressure from your hips. In the event that you remain in forward folding models for some time and spotlight on taking moderate, unfaltering breaths into the zones where you feel the stretch, the vitality that traps dread is discharged from your muscles.

Jewel Fortress (Manipura) Chakra

The third chakra is situated in the navel locale. Its name, manipura, implies "jewel fortress" and wonderfully indicates the fundamental truth that you are a jewel. This chakra relates to self-esteem and mental self-portrait, which we as a whole know is effectively mutilated, in that we overlook what our identity is. Since this is so significant, we rehash it. You're valuable unimaginable; experiences don't modify your substance. At the point when you recall this, you digest educational experiences all the more effectively, and at the point when you don't, you can have blockage in this chakra, which prompts low self-esteem; what's more, trouble tolerating change.

There are two sorts of represents that work on your gut region, or center. Represents that fortify your belly muscles and strengthen this chakra are valuable if your anxiety originates from an inclination or idea that you basically can't manage life. The coming about feeling of solidarity breaks your conviction that you can't adapt. Similarly significant are contorting presents, where you turn your spine first one way and afterward the other, as you do when you turn around and look behind you previously you back your vehicle out of a parking spot. Turning moves vitality through the region of your gut. This encourages you to "digest" experiences, much as you do nourishment, absorbing what you can and proceeding onward out what you can't. On the off chance that you work with this chakra, the subsequent feeling of flexibility is an incredible cure for anxiety caused by natural experiences.

Unstruck (Anahata) Chakra

Fourth is the anahata chakra, situated at the base of the sternum, near your heart. Anahata signifies, 'the unstruck sound." This chakra identifies with the heart, lungs, spleen, and thoracic spine, and reflects intense subject matters. Tightening in this chakra can appear as instability, apprehension, anxiety, and an excessively basic nature. Opening this chakra opens your mental fortitude to pursue your internal direction, and reestablishes your eagerness to go out on a limb with others and feel completely invigorated as a person. Since dread can make you close your heart, it's imperative to empathetically keep your heart open, in light of the fact that a shut heart denies you of the bliss that originates from adoring. Back-twisting stances open and lift your chest, like what you do when you step outside to take a gander at the night sky, put your hands on your hips, and tilt your head back to see the stars straightforwardly overhead. Back-twisting presents, which stretch back your shoulders and uncover your heart, discharge despondency, furthermore, make space for new life. Delicate back-twisting stances are restorative for the anxiety brought about by any conviction or experience that has persuaded you that you can't cherish or be adored.

Qualities Of The Physical Practice Of Yoga

How you practice the poses is as significant as which poses you do. Next are two styles of training that have altogether different outcomes. Contingent upon how you convey anxiety and what's happening in your present life, you may discover one of these moves toward increasingly helpful in lessening anxiety.

Purifying and Cooling

Since anxiety fires up your body and accelerates your breath, yoga poses for anxiety, for the most part, center around cooling the body and hindering your breath. Subsequently, it's useful to move gradually, inhale easily, and continuously permit your body to unwind as you experience your poses. Think about how invigorating an evening rest is or how reviving it is to rest halfway while climbing up a mountain. Both of these exercises quiet and reestablish you. In yoga, purifying systems incorporate bit by bit stretching the out-breath, quickly delaying after breathing out, shutting your eyes during poses, rehearsing helpful forward twists, doing reversals (or topsy turvy poses), and doing some situated or prostrate spinal turns. They lessen unsettling and pressure in the body, and hinder the breath.

Expanding and Warming

On occasion, warmth and exertion are expected to soften pressure. Since quite a while ago, maybe caught strain ought to be met with equivalent power so as to be discharged. You've most likely experienced being worried to such an extent that you needed to go outside and run or do a few physically requesting undertaking. You just needed to go through all the repressed vitality.

In yoga, expanding procedures incorporate keeping your eyes open during poses, moving rapidly, and doing standing poses that fabricate continuance and enthusiastic poses that are stimulating, for example, back curves. On the off chance that you convey a great deal of solid strain, you may profit by starting your training with poses that require quality and perseverance. In the wake of warming the muscles, which defrost pressure, you can, at that point, unwind into all the more quieting yoga poses.

Breathing and the Poses

Whatever type of rehearsing the poses you like, make sure to relax.

Numerous individuals state that what they most convey from yoga class into their everyday lives is the capacity to take full breaths and to concentrate on breathing when they're pushed. In the event that you do the yoga stances without focusing on your breath, you just get halfway advantages. Truth be told, it may be useful to make a sign that says, "Inhale," and prop it up before you to assist you with remaining mindful of your breathing while at the same time doing your poses.

Props and the Poses

We prescribe attempting the poses in this part before putting resources into props to use with your poses. You can undoubtedly substitute regular family unit things for formal props. Utilizing props can incredibly improve the nature of your experience as you do yoga poses. Commonly, yoga props comprise of a yoga tangle, a tie, a square, what's more, a yoga cover, and for helpful yoga, include a support. Be that as it may, you need none to do this yoga for anxiety poses. A long, supple belt or a man's tie works well for a tie. A thick phone directory or collapsed shower towel functions admirably for a square. You can utilize an enormous seashore towel instead of a yoga tangle, and two or three pads will fill in as a reinforce. Before you start your everyday asana practice, have your props or choices close by so you don't need to interfere with your training to discover them. At that point, as your dedication develops, you might need to buy a yoga tangle and different things.

Yoga Poses to Diminish Pressure

Stress decrease poses refine your body as they discharge strain furthermore, relieve trembling. We should start with a "minibreak" present, something you've intuitively done on many occasions. An extraordinary break, despite the fact that it is anything but a conventional yoga represent, it's mitigating and can be done anyplace. It's consoling to take the heaviness of the world off your brain by holding your head with your hands and shutting your eyes. In Yoga as Medicine (2007, 12) Timothy McCall gives these guidelines: "Tenderly move the tissue between your eyebrows toward your nose." Try it, and you'll find that it's unwinding to pull your eyebrows down delicately.

Minibreak Pose

Sit confronting a table or work area. Spot both of your feet on the floor. Put your hands on your brow, with your fingers holding your head also, your palms on your eyebrows. Put both of your elbows, shoulder separation separated, on the table or work area. Close your eyes.

Tenderly press down on your head with your fingers and move your eyebrows somewhat down toward your checks. Spot your mindfulness on your breath and rest in this situation for a few breaths.

Minirest Pose

Spot your lower arms on the table and lay your brow on your arms in "mini rest" present. Tenderly press your eyebrows down toward your cheeks. Concentrate on breathing in and out for a few rounds.

Forward-Folding Poses

Since they're so quieting, forward folds are extraordinary pressure reducers. Poses of contemplation, they have a sense of security since you twist your body into itself. Your midsection and heart are ensured. They, too, stretch the hips, discharge the muscles of your lower back, and open the first chakra territory. Here are two strain diminishing forward folds you can do at home, in your organization's lounge, or in your office.

Buttocks-Against-Wall Forward Fold

Release your belt and garments around the midsection and neck. Take off your shoes. Remain by a divider, confronting the focal point of the room, with your feet hip-width separated, six to eighteen inches from the divider.

Press your rump against the divider. Curve your knees, and let your head hang toward the floor. Lay your hands on the floor, or hold your lower legs or legs with your hands. On the other hand, position a seat before you, and spot your hands on the seat.

Presently you're prepared for the five simple poses.

A Daily Yoga Practice for Anxiety: The Five Easy Poses

The accompanying practice quiets the body and brain. While these five simple poses are useful for assuaging a specific scene of anxiety, they're intended to be an establishment for an everyday practice. In case you're new to yoga, these are extraordinary poses in the first place. They feel better; furthermore, you don't need to be physically fit to start working with them.

They take under fifteen minutes, so they don't require a huge time responsibility. Be that as it may, you do need to rehearse them all together to get the advantages. In the event that you can't do a portion of the poses, essentially skip them. Concentrate on different poses as opposed to attempt to compel your body to accomplish something it can't do.

These five poses are generally simple for most sound bodies.

Simple Pose 1: Bridge Pose

Lie on your back, with your hands stretched out next to your hips and your palms looking up. Curve your knees and spot your feet about six inches from your hips. Keep your feet and knees hip-width separated. Breathe in and lift your hips up. Draw your shoulders close together. Either let your hands stay laying on the floor, or catch your hands together. Push on your shoulders and lift your chest. Hold the posture for six to twelve breaths. Feel the exertion in your posterior and thighs. Delicately endeavor to push your heart toward your jaw and enable your chest to open. Descend and rest for a couple breaths, and afterward embrace your knees to your chest.

Simple Pose 2: Upward-Stretched Legs

Keep your arms by your sides. Raise your legs undetermined and remain for a couple of breaths. At that point, broaden your arms overhead, if it's agreeable, generally leave them at your sides. In the event that it's awkward to fix your legs, twist your knees or spot a hinder under your sacrum. When you're in an agreeable position, concentrate on the in-and-out development of your breath. Hold the posture for six to twelve breaths. Descend and embrace your knees to your chest.

Simple Pose 3: Staff Pose

Sit erect and tall. Put your hands behind your hips to support the extending of your spine and opening of your chest. Fold your jaw toward your chest and look down. Remain there, or in the event that you can, stretch your arms overhead and bring your jaw up so you can look straight ahead. Concentrate on breathing in and out. Hold for six to twelve breaths.

Simple Pose 4: Bound-Angle Pose

Sit with your spine erect. Bring the bottoms of your feet together, serenely near your crotch. Spot your hands behind your hips to support the lifting of your spine. Bow your jawline toward your chest. Remain there for a few breaths.

On the off chance that it's agreeable to do as such, catch your feet with your hands. Bring your jaw to an unbiased position, and either take a gander at the floor a couple of feet before you or close your eyes. Concentrate on breathing in and out for six to twelve breaths.

Simple Pose 5: Child's Pose

Start on your hands and knees. Spot your knees somewhat more extensive than hip-width separated. Protract your bottom back toward your hips, and lower your chest toward your thighs. Rest your arms overhead or at your sides. Spot a collapsed cover under your head for support, whenever wanted. Enable your brow to lay on the cover or floor. On the off chance that this is awkward for your knees, move up a cover and place it on your lower legs, near your knees, for support. Remain there for at least eight breaths Unwind and appreciate.

This closes the five simple poses practice. This is an extraordinary ten-to-fifteen minute practice, which might be sufficient for you, particularly first and foremost. As you want, you can protract your training by just rehashing the five simple poses.

Breath Retention

Breath retention is a strategy for retraining the manner in which you breathe. In this training, you breathe in, purposefully hold your breath, and afterward, breathe out. To make it simple and smooth, facilitate your breathing by rationally checking. Breathe in as you tally to four. Hold your breath for the check of two, and afterward, breathe out as you tally to four. Do this for a couple of rounds until your breath continuously develops.

At that point, breathe in for the check of six, hold your breath as you tally to three, and breathe out as you check to six. Do this for a couple of breaths, insofar as you're loose. At that point, discharge your endeavors, and basically sit and appreciate monitoring the wonderful impressions of breathing for a couple of breaths.

This is a delicate practice, so kindly don't constrain. Whenever there's any hint of trouble, let go of the training and loosen up all endeavors. This isn't expected to expand strain. The objective is moderate and cadenced breathing and diminished strain.

Alternate-Nostril Breathing

Regardless of whether you're mindful of your nasal cycle, you have one.

Your breath alternates between your correct nostril and left nostril for the duration of the day and night. Check for yourself. Close off your left nostril, and breathe in and out through your correct nostril. Presently close off your correct nostril, and breathe in and out through your left nostril.

You presumably see that you're breathing in increasingly through one nostril than the other.

Right-nostril breathing is warming and stimulating. Left-nostril breathing is cooling and helpful. Predominately breathing through the correct nostril triggers the thoughtful sensory system's battle or-flight reaction, and predominately breathing through the left nostril triggers the parasympathetic framework's unwinding reaction. The yogic act of alternate-nostril breathing is accepted to adjust the thoughtful and parasympathetic anxious frameworks just as your general vitality. This is a delicate practice. In the event that you think that it's distressing, take a rest. Take an agreeable situated position. Bring your correct hand near your nose. Delicately close your correct nostril with your thumb, and breathe in through your left nostril. Discharge your thumb, gently spread your left nostril with your last two fingers, and breathe out through your right nostril. Presently breathe in through your correct nostril. Discharge your last two fingers, spread your correct nostril with your thumb, and breathe out through your left nostril. This is one cycle of breathing. Rehash a not many cycles. Notice the quieting impact.

Cooling Penetration

Here's a breathing practice to do when you're pushed or tense. It's an extraordinary small scale pressure break. Since the breath of anxiety is predominately right-nostril breathing, you can invigorate the unwinding reaction by breathing only in through your left nostril and out through your correct nostril for a couple of rounds. At that point, continue ordinary breathing, and know about the development of your breath. Appreciate the basic demonstration of breathing.

Conclusion

You can utilize yoga poses independently, as required, to assuage pain, or gathering them all together practice to bit by bit open and loosen up your body, reestablish your capacity to cherish, and create individual quality. Doing a deliberately chose practice in under fifteen minutes alleviates your body as well as expands the progression of vitality through your body. To expand the advantages of your training, center around your breath while holding the poses, which increments your capacity to think, places your consideration in your body, and brings you into present-minute mindfulness. Include a couple of moments toward the finish of your session to recondition your breath. After some time, the advantages of a day by day practice accumulate as your body discharges collected pressure and unwinds. A sound body not just feels magnificent yet in addition, calms the brain and empowers you to concentrate on what truly matters to you.

CONCLUSION: MEDITATION AND MINDFULNESS FOR ANXIETY

Centering prayer, a meditative method, is a seeking of a true relationship with God or the Ultimate Reality. Take time each day to be with yourself, out of respect for yourself. In this tumultuous, noisy, and active world, you need to be in touch with your deeper self, beyond the ordinary psychological awareness that preoccupies you. —Father Thomas Keating

Meditation is taking some tranquil time to sit; concentrate on your breath, mantra, or stillness; and witness your considerations. When you catch yourself thinking, you basically set your attention back on your breath, mantra, or the quietness in or around you. After some time, contemplations die down, at least for a minute or then again two, and when that happens, you feel peaceful. Any anxiety you feel starts to fade. On the off chance that you meditate as a spiritual practice, as Father Thomas Keating teaches, then those peaceful minutes are an opportunity to connect to higher consciousness.

Meditation trains you to turn out to be increasingly conscious of what's happening in your body and psyche, and teaches you to know about existence right now. Meditation causes you to observe and distinguish thought patterns that contribute to anxiety, and because meditation situates you to the present minute, it sustains and solaces you as only being in the now can do. With the goal that you can watch your mind and avoid becoming mixed up in the past or future, meditation practices give your attention something to concentrate on. And, at the times when your psyche hushes up, you're aware of stillness and experience inward peace.

Withdrawal of the Senses

One way to concentrate is by paying attention to only one of the senses.

A basic way to encounter this is to close your eyes and press your thumbs against the openings of your ears, shutting off your hearing. Murmur tenderly and tune in to the sound of your murmuring. This straightforward exercise centers your awareness on what you hear. Doing so narrows your attention and withdraws your engagement from your general surroundings. Since we take in information from the external world through our tactile capacities, withdrawing your senses means to retreat from active, various tactile sources of info. The restriction can be to one tangible information, for example, gazing at a lit candle, or you can retreat from all tactile inputs. You would start classical yoga meditation by taking asylum from sights, sounds, scents, and activities. This is the reason instructions to meditate start with sitting in calm, still place.

Lying awake in bed around evening time is similar to meditating with your eyes shut.

During the night, your general surroundings are peaceful and, as yet, taking rest. The room is dark, and the encompassing environment retreats from your awareness. You experience withdrawal of the senses, yet you can even now have all sorts of experiences. Your psyche may generate considerations, emotions can arise, and you may have in essence sensations, however then a couple of moments later, you may lie there awake, contented, and peaceful. While both meditating and resting in bed are seasons of minimal tangible info, they have various goals. As you lie in bed, your motivation is rest and no awareness, whereas when you sit for meditation, your purpose is to be awake and aware.

When You're Sleepy

You may feel sleepy during meditation since rest is profoundly associated with tactile withdrawal. Don't be discouraged if this happens, because it may indicate that you need more rest. See what happens when you witness the lethargy. You may find something intriguing about yourself, and on the off chance that you snooze off, it's no serious deal. Sooner or later, you wake up again. Another option is to meditate with your eyes open, gazing softly at the floor or some article, since open eyes are associated with alertness.

Concentration

When you concentrate, you direct your attention to something specific. Like a laser beam, you home in, aiming to stay focused. Concentration involves intention, and is the opposite of drifting or distracted attention. The yogis of the East taught that a preliminary stage of meditation is teaching the mind to be fully engrossed in a single focus. Developing the capacity to concentrate takes some practice, but the benefits are well worth the effort, because concentration calms your restless mind, which is great medicine for the worried mind that jumps hither and yon.

You prepare for concentration by sitting in a quiet room. Absence of external stimulation makes it easier to train your mind to become one-pointed. The next step is to give your attention something to focus on. Breath and mantra are two great choices for concentration. Breathing is essential to life, and mantra aligns you with higher consciousness — experiment with both to find which is more appealing. Most likely, you'll gravitate toward one. Go with what works naturally for you. Make your practice enjoyable so that you don't want to skip out on it.

Concentration consists of focusing, discovering when you're not focusing, and returning to your desired focus. Having something to concentrate on is like having an anchor to the present moment. When you realize you've drifted off into thoughts, put your awareness back on whatever you're focusing on, and once again, you'll be alert and aware. It's like saying, "Oops, I drifted away, and here I am again."

Focusing on the Breath

The breath is wonderful to focus on, because putting your attention on breathing tends to slow it down, which triggers the relaxation response. Also, as long as you live, you breathe, so breath is readily available. You can pay attention anytime you like. Focusing on the breath as you meditate trains you to be more aware of your breathing in general, which has two effects: your breath evens out, becoming more rhythmic, and you find yourself being aware of your breathing off and on throughout your day. You literally begin to experience your breath as an intimate friend, always there. There's no one way to attune your awareness to your breath.

Experiment to find a way to become aware of your breath that feels right for you. One suggestion is that if you're new to meditation, you may find it comforting to focus your attention on the movement of air going in and out of your nostrils. The nostrils are a distinct and specific area to focus on. The nostril openings are at the surface of the skin, and focusing on that area can feel safe if you're uncomfortable tuning into sensations inside your body.

You may also focus your awareness on the breath in your chest area, inside your body. Put your attention on the movement of your ribs. Feel them expand as breath comes in, and contract as breath goes out. Another way is to focus exclusively on your abdomen. Feel it rise and fall in response to your breath. The belly area is larger and less distinct than the nostrils, and involves a diffuse, soft focus. Alternatively, you may find it appealing to follow the breath's entire journey as it travels in and out of your body.

Focusing on a Mantra

Focusing on a mantra is equally wonderful. When you fill your mind with the words and sounds of higher consciousness, you align yourself with wisdom, love, and peace, which soothe your body and mind, and expand your perspective. Silently repeat your preferred word for the divine, such as the Hebrew word *abba*, meaning "father," or use a word that represents some spiritual quality, such as "mercy."

Meditating Relieves Anxiety

When you suffer from anxiety, meditation can be your lifeline. Although you may initially flounder a little with how to do it, once you're comfortable with meditation, you'll return to it daily. It becomes a sanctuary, a place of refuge.

You gladly go to your chair or meditation cushion, because you know its benefits.

At the very least, meditation is a relief from busyness. You're taking time to be with yourself. While meditating, you usually sit in a quiet room to give yourself a break from overstimulation and overactivity. As such, it's relieving, even though your mind occasionally generates thoughts. On noisy-mind days, focus on your breath or your mantra, watch what your mind is doing, and enjoy the moments when there's less mind chatter. While some meditation sessions are more enjoyable than others, none are worthless. On the days when your mind is less active, enjoy your peaceful state.

After you've obtained some experience meditating, you can access inner stillness, even if only for a moment. Here's how it happens: You begin your practice the way you usually do, by focusing on your breath or reciting your mantra, and then all becomes quiet. For as long as it lasts, you connect with stillness. The next thing you realize is that your mind tosses out a few thoughts and recaptures your attention. The moments and minutes when you fall into deep quiet are fortunate, because in that quiet space, anxiety dissolves, and you feel incredible peace.

Meditating on Your Heart

When you need tender support, focus on your heart chakra. In *The Heart of Meditation*, Swami Durgananda (2002, 220) says that the heart center is "where the inhalation comes to rest…beneath the breastbone, four to five inches below the collarbone." In this meditation, focus on the breath flowing in and out of your heart center. Swami Durgananda instructs you to even "enter the space inside the heart center. You may sit with your hands in a prayer pose, place your right hand over your heart, or fold your hands on your lap. Do what's comfortable and natural. If you like, breathe kindness into and out of your heart. Feel the radiant warmth of your heart. Connect with the compassion you feel. Let yourself be held in the embrace of your heart. This is a wonderful meditation for comforting yourself. While doing a research project, our friend Hal read in *The Biology of Transcendence*, by Joseph Pearce (2002), that the cells of the heart muscle are 60 percent nerve cells (as in the brain), and in the first moments after conception, they exhibit life and movement. Miraculously, mysteriously, they take on a rhythm of their own, which they maintain until you die. After completing his research, Hal had heart surgery. Afterward, he had a sense of being "disconnected" in ways he'd never before experienced. Knowing that his heart had been momentarily stopped during surgery and that a heart-lung machine had maintained his life, he wondered if he had lost touch with the greater source in the process. During his recovery period, he did heart meditations and made a breakthrough discovery. While meditating, he searched for the source of his heartbeat and held the image of connecting with that greater source. After several days of this meditation, he had powerful experiences of oneness with the infinite. You may want to sense into the mystery of your heartbeat so that meditating on your heart also connects you with your original source.

Mindfulness Practice

You don't have to separate your meditation practice from your daily life. You can witness your thoughts and focus on your breath or mantra whenever you remember to. Practicing meditation in this way during the day is called "mindfulness practice." To make this clearer for you, let's define "mindfulness."A simple definition is "nonjudgmental acceptance of things as they arise in the present moment." It involves noticing what's happening inside and outside of you so you can see things as they are. An easy example is relating to your worrisome thoughts mindfully, which is simply responding to them the same way you do when you meditate. When worry arises, witness it, and place your attention on your breath. When you notice a thought like, *Oh no, what's going to happen?* recognize it as a thought and return your focus to your breath. Taking a breath is nourishing and reorients you to what you're doing and where you are. Breathing intentionally pops you out of your thought trance and provides immediate relief, because it puts some space between you and your fretting.

Mindfulness, or nonjudgmental witnessing, is a tall order because it entails getting in touch with what you experience moment to moment. You can only witness what you allow yourself to be aware of. As someone who's prone to anxiety, you have a natural tendency to want to detach or escape from it, and now you're being counseled to get in touch with it, to witness it.

Putting It All Together with Breath Awareness

Mindfulness puts you in touch with life, and focusing on breathing is the lifeline that enables you to do this. For that reason, breath awareness is central to mindfulness. It puts you back in your body and gets you out of your thoughts. If you don't want to miss out on life, practice being aware of your breath coming in and going out. You know what it's like to watch a movie and become distracted by worrying about tomorrow. You miss an entire conversation on the screen, and then refocus on the screen and try to figure out what's going on. You turn to your friend, who's also watching, and ask, "What did he say?" Your friend answers your question, and you both miss the ongoing conversation between the actors. Now two people are scrambling to catch up with the movie. Now let's say that you watch the movie and practice mindfulness. Most of your attention is on what you see and hear on the screen, and a small part of your attention focuses on your breath's in-and-out movement. As a result, you're less likely to be taken away by your thoughts, but when you do, you more quickly realize it. Focusing on the continuous flow of breath keeps you observant, preventing you from becoming consumed by thinking. So not only do you suffer less from fretting about the next day, but you also avoid missing as much of the movie or diverting your friend's attention away from the screen.

Walking a Path of Mindfulness

A lovely form of mindfulness practice is walking meditation. In this meditation, you walk slowly, take small steps, and coordinate your movement with your breath. Take a few steps on each in-breath and each out-breath. Let your breath be comfortable. Notice each foot as it steps. Feel where your feet touch the ground or floor. Pay attention to how your heel steps down, how your foot rolls, and how you push off from the front of your foot with each step. Paying attention like this helps you to be in the present moment rather than get ahead of yourself. Enjoy breathing and walking.

Do this leisurely, slowly. Relax as you stroll.

Walk to walk! You're not hurrying to some destination, wandering mindlessly, or getting exercise. You're paying attention to your experience in the present moment while walking. When practicing outdoors, look around as you slowly walk. Feel the air movement and the temperature. Take in the sights and sounds while coordinating breath with movement. This trains you to be aware of what's happening in you and what's going on around you in the present moment.

We love to walk in the woods and study the trees and leaves, touching bark, smelling vegetation, and watching the rays of sunlight flicker through the leaves.

Another favorite is stepping outdoors on the deck and watching crows, hawks, and turkey buzzards fly overhead. Rick shows Mary the different flying techniques of the birds, and we stand transfixed for a moment, absorbed in the present moment. Sometimes we stroll over to the fishpond and watch the goldfish. When we go back inside to our home office, we feel refreshed and soothed. Mary occasionally mindfully walks to and from the restroom when she's working at her counseling office. You can practice mindful walking in any location, and it's beneficial to practice even for a few moments.

Practicing walking meditation indoors is a great alternative to nervous pacing. Intentional focusing makes all the difference. Breathe out, take three small steps, and look at the floor. Breathe in, take three small steps, and notice colors. And on you go, observing and striding. Continue walking until you feel calm, which is how you'll know that you've engaged the relaxation response.

Implementing Mindfulness

Practicing all the elements of mindfulness—being aware of breathing, allowing, noticing, naming your inner experience, and taking in the details of your surroundings—results in your living in life's present, moment-to-moment unfolding. Of course, that's easier said than done! Fortunately, you have endless opportunities to practice, and practicing is quite fun. Here's how you do it. When you brush your teeth, notice where your toothbrush is in your mouth, feel its pressure, taste the toothpaste, notice your saliva, and, of course, notice that you're breathing in and out. When thoughts arise, name them "thinking." When you feel rushed, name this experience "rushing."That's a lot to be conscious of! In the beginning, practice mindfulness when you're doing enjoyable tasks to make it easy to stay in the experience. It doesn't matter if you practice while driving the car, drinking coffee, taking a shower, or walking around the block.

What matters is that you practice. After some practice, experiment with tasks that you typically don't enjoy. You'll discover something very relieving: the task isn't as tedious or unpleasant as you thought it would be. You'll just do what you do, and who knows? Since you'll be calm, you might find more enjoyable ways to do what needs to be done.

Conclusion

As simple as meditation and mindfulness are, these practices can be personally challenging. Approach these skills as if you were learning a new dance step, mastering a piece of music, or refining your table-tennis skills. Give yourself some time, and understand that your efforts are beneficial and don't depend on any certain experience in meditation. If your mind is busy, you're enhancing your ability to concentrate and witness. If your mind is quiet, you access inner

quiet and calm. As Father Thomas Keating said to Mary, "God appreciates all efforts at friendship." We encourage you to keep your appointment with meditation. Give a little of yourself and your time to meditation, and it will give you much in return.